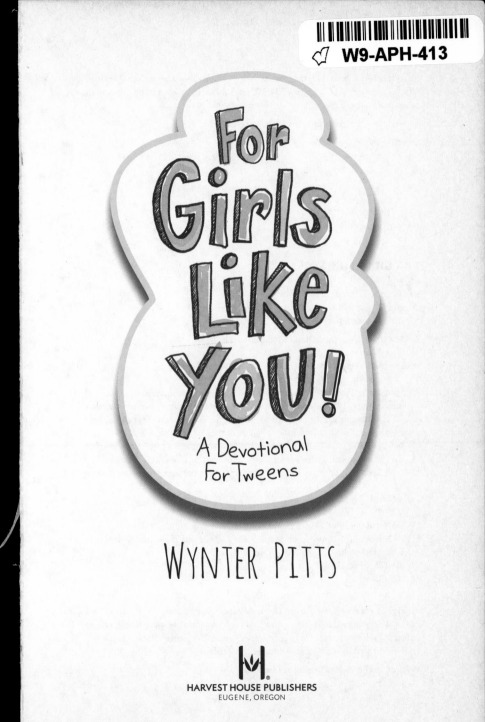

For Girls Like You!

A Devotional For Tweens

WYNTER PITTS

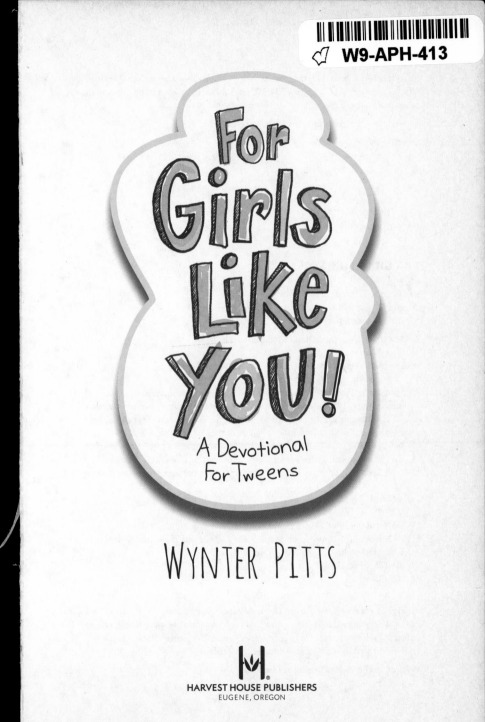

HARVEST HOUSE PUBLISHERS
EUGENE, OREGON

Cover by www.DesignByJulia.com, Woodland Park, CO

Cover illustration © blue67design / Shutterstock

FOR GIRLS LIKE YOU

Copyright © 2015 Wynter Pitts
Published by Harvest House Publishers
Eugene, Oregon 97402
www.harvesthousepublishers.com

Library of Congress Cataloging-in-Publication Data
Pitts, Wynter, author.
For girls like you / Wynter Pitts.
pages cm
Summary: "Tween girls have access to an unbelievable amount of media and information with just a simple click of the remote or mouse. Every outlet they turn to attempts to subtly influence their worldview...and what they believe about themselves directly affects how they live. Wynter Pitts, founder of *For Girls Like You* magazine, gives girls a new devotional showing them a correct definition of themselves, opening their eyes to God's truth and the difference it makes in their lives. Each daily devotion includes a prayer to help girls apply the lesson."—Provided by publisher.
Audience: Ages 8-12.
ISBN 978-0-7369-6175-2 (pbk.)
ISBN 978-0-7369-6176-9 (eBook)
1. Christian life—Juvenile literature. 2. Girls—Religious life—Juvenile literature. 3. Conduct of life—Juvenile literature. I. Title.
BV4551.3.P58 2015
248.8'2—dc23

2014022678

Printed in the United States of America

15 16 17 18 19 20 21 22 / VP-JH / 10 9 8 7 6 5 4 3

Hello to you! Yes, you, sitting right there...the one holding this book!

Guess what? I have some things I want to tell you.

I want you to know that every single page of this book is for you!

Yes, it is a devotional and you may think that sounds like a book for your mom or another adult. Well, it's not! This is a devotional for you.

It is special. It is a book about God's heart and your life.

You may not always understand everything you read in the Bible. When I was a little girl I didn't! But I thought that one day the Bible would make total sense to me. When I was all grown up, of course.

I was wrong. God's words, written in the Bible, are for everyone, at every age!

God knows all about friendships. He knows all about beauty, hard work, fear, love, and fun! He knows all about everything because He created it all.

God wants you to know all about Him and how His love will change your life!

So for the next few weeks, every day, can you find a quiet spot and grab a Bible and a pen so we can talk about God and life?

Are you ready to see what God wants you to know? Let's get started!

The Big Deal with a Little Hamster

I am not a fan of mice! I am not talking about the kind that are stuffed with cotton, have big black circles for ears, and live in a magical castle at an amusement park, like Mickey Mouse. I am thinking of the kind that squeak around dark rooms and nibble on your leftover crackers. The creepy little furry ones!

I will admit that just thinking about their dark marble eyes, thin whiskers, pointy noses, big teeth, and long skinny tails totally grosses me out! In fact, I feel the exact same way about hamsters, gerbils, and rats. They all give me chills.

So would you believe me if I told you that I once had a pet hamster?

It is true. You can also believe me when I say I was totally grossed out by him too. So you are probably wondering why I even had one, right?

When I was a little girl, my brother had a lot of animals and pets. Somehow he managed to talk our mother into letting him have everything from baby lizards and hermit crabs to sharks!

But guess what animal he never asked for?

You got it. A hamster.

I did not enjoy having a hamster. I didn't

like feeding him, playing with him, or looking at him. But I wanted to have a pet so bad that I let a creepy furry little creature live in my room! It may seem weird but all I really wanted was to be like my brother—I wanted to fit in.

Please tell me that I am not alone. Have you ever done something just to try to be like someone else?

Maybe you have never owned a hamster, but maybe you talked your mom into letting you buy a certain shirt, watch a certain movie, or hang out with a certain person. Maybe you enjoyed it but maybe you were just doing it to try to fit in.

God knew that wanting to fit in and be like everyone else would be hard, so He talks about it a lot in the Bible!

Romans 12:2 says, "Do not conform to the pattern of this world, but be transformed by the renewing of your mind."

This just means that we should not try to fit in or be like someone else. We should only want to be like Jesus and do and have what He says is good for us! When you try to be like Jesus, you don't have to worry about fitting in. You can just be you!

Can you think of a time that you wanted to fit in? What can you do today to try to be more like Christ?

Dear God, I am so glad You know what is best for me. Please help me to not try to be like other people. I want to be like You! In Jesus's name, amen.

Perfectly Imperfect

Raise your hand if you are perfect!

Are you jumping out of your seat, eagerly waving your hand in the air? Or are you keeping it down, shamefully buried in your lap? Or maybe you are a little confused and not really sure what to do.

No matter how you feel, you should know that wanting to be perfect and never getting there is totally normal. Actually, God already knows that you aren't perfect, and you do not need to feel ashamed when you fail.

The Bible says that the only perfect person who will ever live is Jesus. It also says that if you love Jesus you should want to be like Him.

That is a little confusing, right? *How can you be like Jesus when He is perfect...and you're not?* Here is what you need to know: Being perfect is Jesus's job. Your job is to love Him and to love others the way He would want you to! Jesus wants you to be like Him, but He also knows that you cannot do that without His help and His love. When you trust Jesus and let His love come inside of you, He will help you be the best that you can be!

The Bible says, "Love the Lord your God with all your heart and with all your soul and with all your mind and with all your strength [and] love your neighbor as yourself" (Mark 12:30-31).

This means that there is no need to stress about getting perfect grades, having perfect hair, or being a perfect friend. It's impossible! It does not mean that you shouldn't try your best. But your biggest job is to focus on how you can love God more in your heart and show that love through how you treat other people. His love takes care of everything else.

Loving God with your whole heart is what makes you want to be like Jesus...just how God wants you! Can you think of a way that you can love Jesus more today? Is there something you can do or someone you can help to show God your love for Him today?

Dear God, thank You for Your love and reminding me today that even though I can't be perfect, You love me perfectly. Help me to love You with all of me! Help me to love others like You love them. In Jesus's name, amen.

I went to a very small school and I was friends with everyone in my class. But just like most girls, I definitely had a few BEST friends! One of my best friends was Michell. Michell and I did everything together! We sat next to each other in class, ate lunch together, begged our families for sleepovers, and sometimes we even went along on each other's family vacations!

I will never forget this one family vacation. We were thrilled to be together...until around the middle of our trip. We were at the pool and Michell and I had a huge fight—in front of everyone! It was so embarrassing! But even worse than that, after it was all over my mom separated us. I felt horrible. I missed my friend and I felt guilty for treating her so badly.

After a while, I just could not take it anymore. It just did not feel great to know that I had been so unkind to someone I loved. I knew what I had to do. I finally built up enough courage to find her and ask her to forgive me. After a long pause, she did. I was thrilled to have things back to normal with my best friend! I felt free and happy again because Michell chose to stop being upset because of how I treated her. She chose to love me instead.

You see, the word *forgive* really means that you change your bad feelings and attitude toward someone who upset you or mistreated you. Do you know that when you confess your sins, God always forgives you? The Bible says that "as far as the east is from the west, so far has [God] removed our transgressions from us" (Psalm 103:12).

The word *transgressions* means *sin*, and this verse simply means that when we sin or do something wrong, God will forgive us. When we go to Him and admit that we haven't been perfect, He takes away all of our shame and feelings of guilt!

God's forgiveness is forever. If you and your friend were standing on a line and you walked to the left and your friend walked to the right, you would continue to get further and further apart. When God forgives us, that is what happens with us and our sin. God forgets our sin and pushes it to the left and we continue to walk right, toward Him. If you ever get discouraged and think that God is upset at you, if you have asked Him for forgiveness, you can trust that this scripture is for you and you are forgiven!

Today, think about the many times that God has forgiven you. How does it make you feel?

Dear God, I am grateful that You do not let the things I do wrong push me away from You, but instead, You forgive me when I ask and bring me closer to You. Help me to believe that I am forgiven regardless of how bad a mistake I make. Thank You for forgiveness! In Jesus's name, amen.

Do you know that God is everywhere?

He is not just with the adults in church on Sunday mornings or at the kitchen table when you say your grace before dinner. Yes, He is there during those times, but there is so much more to God's presence than we sometimes realize.

Does it surprise you to know that God is with you at school while you hang out with your friends and while you are sitting in your classroom? God is even right there with you when you are home, alone in your room, reading a book, or watching TV. The best part is, at the same time that He is with you, He is everywhere else...around the entire world.

The Bible tells us that God is *omnipresent*. That big word simply means that God is present everywhere—all of the time. God sees all, knows all, and is always with His children.

Can you think of a time that you were afraid but felt safer when you found out that someone else was in the room with you?

Or have you ever changed your actions or attitude because you realized someone was watching you and you only wanted them to see you on your best behavior?

Maybe simply being around a certain person makes you happy or makes you feel silly or excited?

Let God be that person! When you know that God is with you, you should feel safer, behave better, and smile more! He is always ready to help, protect, comfort, and celebrate with you. He is even with you when you choose to ignore Him. And when needed, He is also there to correct and to teach you. Your job is to accept His love and to see Him in your life every day, everywhere.

Today, will you choose to acknowledge God's presence in every situation? He is always there, waiting and ready to be noticed.

Dear God, thank You for being with me! Help me to remember that You love to take care of me because I am Your special creation! I will not be afraid because You promise to protect me. I am not lonely because You are with me. I do not have to worry because You care for me! In Jesus's name, amen.

Being Me and Being You

Do you know that there are over 7 billion people in this world and that God created every one of them? A number that big is probably hard to imagine, but think about how long it would take you to count that high.

1, 2, 3, 4, 5...forever!

Now, think about how each number from 0 to 1 billion is completely different from the number before it. This is how God created each of us. Of all the people God created, there is no one else exactly like you!

Seriously...how totally awesome and amazing is that! Just think about it—God did not make you just like somebody else but He took His time, focused on every little detail, and made you unique. Everything about you was done on purpose.

If you have ever tried to be like someone else...well, you are not alone. I think at one point in life, everyone has been tempted to laugh just like their BFF, dress like the girl on a certain television show, or dance just like their big sister! You may have even wanted to be able to sing, play a certain sport, or write like someone else.

While admiring others for their unique gifts is not all bad, it's important to know that you were created by God to be you! And when He created you, He had special things that He made you to do. No one else can do them like you.

First Corinthians 12:4-6 says, "There are different kinds of gifts, but the same Spirit distributes them. There are different kinds of service, but the same Lord. There are different kinds of working, but in all of them and in everyone it is the same God at work."

All these gifts have a common origin, but are handed out one by one by the Spirit of God. He decides who gets what and when.

We all have special talents and things we enjoy. And do you know what? God knows what they are...even if we don't! So don't stress about it if you can't think of anything right now. Just pray and ask God to help you figure it out! And while you are waiting, don't be afraid to try new things. Have fun and enjoy what He has given you today!

Dear God, thank You for making me! Help me to know that You made me different from other people on purpose. My skills, gifts, and talents are all very special and unique! Thank You! In Jesus's name, amen.

It Is Not Normal

A miracle is an unusual and wonderful event that cannot be explained by normal activity. Science does not create miracles, and neither do magicians. Miracles are performed by God, and the Bible is full of wonderful examples!

Miracles help us to see God's love for us and His power. In the Bible, God amazed people with events that no one else could explain.

For example, in John 11 the Bible tells the story of a man named Lazarus. Lazarus was sick and his sisters sent for Jesus to come and heal him. But by the time Jesus arrived, Lazarus had already died. Many, including Lazarus's sisters, thought that Jesus had failed them by letting him die. However, when Jesus arrived He went to the tomb and called out his name. Instantly Lazarus came alive again! This showed God's power even over death. That was definitely a miracle.

Matthew 14 describes another miracle. One day 5,000 people gathered to listen and learn from Jesus and His disciples. After being there a long time, the people began to get hungry. All that was available to eat was five loaves of bread and two fish. There is no way that this small amount of food would feed 5,000 people. But God did it! He turned two fish and five loaves into a feast large enough to feed everyone. The Bible says the food never stopped coming!

Amazing, right?

Do you know that Jesus still performs miracles today?

What unusual and wonderful events have happened or are happening to you or around you? Sometimes we get so used to good things happening around us that we forget to see it as an unusual act or a miracle from God!

Look for a miracle today. Not just for yourself but for a friend, family member, or even a stranger! Wait for God to surprise you with something unusual and great. Something that only He can do!

Dear God, thank You for reminding me that You can do anything. Help me to not limit You to what I can explain, and help me to see Your unusual and wonderful miracles each and every day! In Jesus's name, amen.

It's in There

The Bible is the best book you will ever read! If you don't believe me, you should find one, open it, and start reading. Each page is full of exciting, fascinating, and true stories. The kinds of stories that make you want to spend time with the author and tell your friends about how amazing and awesome it was! Stories that teach you how to be a better friend, a helpful sibling, a grateful daughter, and a happy girl!

But here's the best part. The Bible is not just full of stories; it is full of God's words. They are not just stories written by people for fun or pretend, but the Bible is a book from God for your life. It is here to teach you more about Him.

There are answers to your hardest questions, advice on how to handle difficult times, and solutions to every problem. You will never experience anything that God has not already talked about in the Bible!

If you are the kind of girl who likes scientific adventures, you should start right at the beginning with Genesis. After all, God is the creator of the universe! Do you enjoy reading about friendships? Then open up the book of Ruth and read how Ruth and Naomi became best friends during a difficult time and how nothing could destroy their relationship. If you want to read stories of true love and risky adventure, then make your way to the New Testament and open up to Acts and

Romans. There you will read about Paul and how his love for Jesus sent him on a journey with many twists and turns.

Actually, no matter what book of the Bible you turn to, you are reminded of how much God loves you and how much He is willing to do to you, for you, and through you when you choose to follow Him! He wants you to know Him, enjoy Him, and love Him.

The Bible is God's book to you. It's not too big or too long. Find a quiet spot. Read carefully and turn the pages one at a time. Your Bible ends with the book of Revelation, but God wants to continue His story in you! If you already read your Bible, I encourage you to continue reading and looking deeper into what God is saying. If you have never opened your Bible, why don't you begin an amazing journey and start today? If you don't own a Bible, who can you ask to help you find one? Can your mom or dad help? Or is there someone in your church, school, or neighborhood who might have an extra one?

Which book of the Bible will you start reading today?

Dear God, thank You for the Bible! Will You help me learn about You from the stories written in it? Help me to always remember that the Bible is my special book written by You to me! In Jesus's name, amen.

Maybe you have never read a Bible or maybe you read it all of the time. Either way, here are five Bible reading tips to help you!

1. Starting from the beginning of a book, like Genesis or Matthew, will help you better understand the entire book.

2. A study Bible is one that has helpful notes, facts, and sometimes even maps and timelines that can give you better understanding if you are confused.

3. Reading along with a friend, either together or just at the same speed, can help you to stick with it and get the most out of your reading. If you know your friend is going to be reading the same thing as you on the same day, you are more likely to make sure that you read as well!

4. Make sure to take notes. Write down your questions. If you see a verse that you think God might be using to help you or remind you of something, make sure to underline it or write it down.

5. Psalm 34:8 says, "Taste and see that the LORD is good; blessed is the one who takes refuge in him." God is telling us to taste, or try out, His Word. That means to not only get to know it but use it in your life. With every verse you read, ask God to help you make changes in your life that honor Him and grow you to be more like Jesus.

Wanting It All

I love doll babies! No, I do not play with them (*that much*) anymore, but as a little girl I would spend hours playing with my dolls. I had all kinds of dolls: big dolls, little dolls, and dolls that talked. I even had a doll that could write her name!

I do not have any sisters and when I played, my dolls were all mine. I loved it that way! However, it did make it difficult to share when friends visited.

One time, while a few of my dolls and I were visiting my grandparents' home, my grandmother invited another little girl over to play. She was very nice and we were having a lot of fun...until she asked to play with my dolls.

Uh oh. We had a problem. I did *not* want to share.

Seeing that I was having trouble sharing, my grandfather had me line the dolls up. Then he told me to choose which ones I wanted to play with first and to leave the rest of the dolls on the wall for my new friend to enjoy. He explained that after a little while we could switch the dolls or even find a way to play together. Sounded like a good plan, right?

Wrong.

I knelt down next to my dolls, pointed at them one by one, and chose them all! I then stood against the wall and looked down at the floor. I knew my grandparents were disappointed with me and my new friend had tears in her eyes.

I made the choice not to share but it did not make me happy. I had what I wanted but I felt alone and ashamed.

The thing is, I knew better and I knew that God did not want me to be selfish. Being selfish is easy but it does not feel great at all. I could not enjoy my dolls knowing how sad I made everyone else feel. Sharing and giving up something I wanted was hard, but it would have felt so much better.

God wants us to always put others first.

The Bible says, "Do nothing out of selfish ambition or vain conceit. Rather, in humility value others above yourselves" (Philippians 2:3).

Sharing what we have or what is special to us is a way that we show God's love to someone else. It's also how we show God that we are thankful for what He has given us. God shares everything with us! He even shared His own Son, Jesus! If God can share and give us so many wonderful things, He wants us to do the same thing.

What can you choose to share today?

Dear God, help me to not be selfish and to be willing to share with others in need. Please show me how to share like You shared Jesus. In Jesus's name, amen.

Keep Playing

What if real life was like a video game and you could control everything that happened? You would be able to choose your characters, start over whenever you wanted to, or even turn it off if you got tired! You would never have to deal with anything too hard or challenging because you could just skip that part of the game!

That would be perfect—right?

Maybe there is something happening right now and you wish that you could push a button and make it go away. Like that math worksheet that you just can't seem to figure out, or the fight you had with a friend. Well, I am sorry to tell you, but life is not a video game and sometimes you will have to keep playing even when it's no longer fun or when it's really hard to move on to the next part. No matter how tired you get or how hard a situation is, you just have to keep going!

Or maybe there is something bad or scary that has happened to your family or to someone you love and you just can't seem to understand it. Have you ever wondered, "Why does God let bad things happen?"

I am so sorry but I do not have the answer to that question. We may never really understand why certain things happen. Sometimes bad things happen as a result of something someone does or a choice they make, but sometimes it's not anyone's fault and cannot be explained.

But can I tell you what I do know?

God's love is still there even when something bad is happening. He has not forgotten you. He wants you to know that He cares about everything you go through. And even though it does not feel good, God wants you to come to Him for comfort even if you don't understand what He is doing. The Bible says that God's plans always work out! "The LORD is close to the brokenhearted and saves those who are crushed in spirit" (Psalm 34:18).

The Bible also says that God's plan is good, even when it doesn't seem to be: "And we know that in all things God works for the good of those who love him, who have been called according to his purpose" (Romans 8:28).

So yes, bad things do happen. But God is right there, always willing to comfort you and to help you get through it. He knows what He is doing!

Dear God, help me trust Your plans and know that You are with me, even during bad times. Help me keep going! In Jesus's name, amen.

You Win

Some people think that loving God means that life will be easy. But the truth is that there will always be people and things that will try to get in the way and stop you from loving God!

If you open your Bible and read anywhere from Genesis to Revelation (that's from the beginning to the end!) you will come across many battles, fights, and even wars between people, families, and entire countries. They fought over many things, but mostly they fought because some people disagreed with how God's people lived.

For example, in the book of Acts we meet a man named Paul. Paul loved God and believed that Jesus was God's Son. Paul was not trying to hurt anyone, but instead he wanted everyone to know about the forgiveness and love that Jesus promises to give. Sounds like good news, right? But it made some people so upset that they treated Paul very badly. They put him in jail and beat him up!

But bad people and bad situations never stopped Paul from doing what God told him to do. He trusted God and loved Him so much that he was willing to fight for Him.

Paul just kept on teaching people about Jesus, and God wants you to do the very same thing. You may not go to jail for loving and sharing about Jesus with other people, but people will make fun of you or try to stop you. It may be a friend who wants you to do something wrong or it may be a teacher who does not know the truth about God.

Pleasing God is always best, but it is not always popular. The Bible says to be courageous and strong and to continue to do what God tells you. He promises that you will win!

First Chronicles 28:20 says, "Be strong and courageous, and do the work. Do not be afraid or discouraged, for the LORD God, my God, is with you. He will not fail you or forsake you until all the work for the service of the temple of the LORD is finished."

So the question is—do you love God enough to fight for Him?

Dear God, I know that You are always fighting for me. Thank You for giving me Jesus. Please help me be strong and courageous as I live for You today. Help me not to be afraid of telling others about You. Help me do the *right* thing, not the popular thing. Thank You for protecting me! In Jesus's name, amen.

What God Thinks About You

This may be the first time you have heard this or it may just be a reminder, but there is something I want you to know. God loves you and He wants you to know how special and wonderful you are!

Here is something else you should know: You are not special because of how great your hair looks, how smart you are, or even because you are really nice. You are special because God chose you, and He created you to live for Him.

God picked out everything about you and made you exactly how He wanted you. It does not always feel that way because what other people say and think about you can be confusing and distract you. Distractions keep you from seeing the truth!

God knew that this would happen, so He put a few reminders of what He thinks about you in the Bible. Here they are:

God made you wonderful! "I praise you because I am fearfully and wonderfully made" (Psalm 139:14).

God knows everything about you and He cares about you! "And even the very hairs of your head are all numbered. So don't be afraid; you are worth more than many sparrows" (Matthew 10:30-31).

You are His creation and He has a plan for you! "For we are God's handiwork, created in Christ

Jesus to do good works, which God prepared in advance for us to do" (Ephesians 2:10).

The same God that created this entire world also created *you*! The color of your hair, the color of your skin, how tall you are, how loud you laugh, and the sound of your voice. God did it all on purpose and made you just the way you are so that you can love and serve Him! No matter what you feel like or what people say, remember these verses and the truth about yourself!

Dear God, thank You for creating me! Thank You for the reminders that You put in the Bible. Help me to always believe what You say about me and not what others think about me. In Jesus's name, amen.

A Princess Is Born

Have you ever watched a princess movie and wondered what it would be like to be a king's daughter or part of a royal family? The dresses, the fancy dinners, and the balls...it all looks so fun, doesn't it?

Did you know that you are the daughter of a King? Yes, you are—the King of the Universe. You are God's daughter, my friend, and that makes you royalty!

Now, your life may look different from that of a princess in the movies. Choosing a dress and planning fancy parties is fun, but your Father, the King, has other, bigger plans for you. (Don't worry, that doesn't mean you can't plan parties and wear fancy dresses too!)

The Bible says, "You are a chosen people, a royal priesthood, a holy nation, God's special possession, that you may declare the praises of him who called you out of darkness into his wonderful light" (1 Peter 2:9).

Not sure what a "royal priesthood" means? In the Bible, a priest had a lot of jobs, but his two main jobs were to share God's message with others and to talk to God for other people. He had to have a really close relationship with God.

Because you are a part of God's royal family, you get to talk to God for yourself. At any time you can tell Him how you are feeling and thank

Him for what He is doing. You can ask Him for help and for things you need and want.

But your relationship with God is not just about you. He wants you to share His message of love and grace with other people too! His message is shared when you tell others about Jesus, serve other people, and teach people things you have come to know about God as you grow.

Always remember that as the King's daughter, people are looking to you to see what God looks like. Never forget to take time to talk to God for yourself and for others.

Dear God, thank You for allowing me to have such a close relationship with You. Help me stay close to You all the time so I know what You want me to say and do. In Jesus's name, amen.

Honestly Speaking

Let's be honest. I am sure you can think of a time when telling a lie seemed like a good idea or the easiest way to get out of something. Right? Maybe you were just trying to avoid getting in trouble or trying to cover up a bad decision, and it seemed like a lie would make it all disappear.

I am also pretty sure you can think of a time when you were affected by someone else's choice to tell a lie. Maybe your little brother or sister blamed you for something they did or a classmate made up a story about you. Do you remember how that made you feel?

Lies hurt, and it doesn't matter which end of the story you are on. They hurt the people we tell them to and they hurt the person telling them, and whether or not anyone ever finds out really doesn't matter. It is important to be a person of integrity, honesty, and truth!

Telling the truth is an important part of becoming more like Jesus and creating good habits. Actually, the Bible tells us that God does not enjoy being with people who tell lies!

The Bible says, "The LORD detests lying lips, but he delights in people who are trustworthy" (Proverbs 12:22). We are also told to "put off falsehood and speak truthfully to your neighbor, for we are all members of one body" (Ephesians 4:25). What this adds up to, then, is this: no more lies, no more pretense.

Tell your neighbor the truth. In Christ's body we're all connected to each other, after all. When you lie to others, you end up lying to yourself.

The next time you find yourself having to choose between sticking to the truth or telling a lie, ask God to help you be honest and brave enough to tell the truth!

Dear God, even if it makes me look not-so-good, I want You to look good, so help me to always be honest and sincere. Please help me see how always telling the truth will be good for me even if it does not feel good in the moment. In Jesus's name, amen.

That Is Too Much

I love shoes. All kinds of shoes! Boots. Sandals. Sneakers. High heels. Black, brown, colorful...I love them all!

If you were to look in my closet you would see that I am telling you the truth. You would also see that my love for shoes sometimes causes a bit of a messy situation. I only have two feet! That means that every day I have a lot of shoes that I am not wearing, tossed all over the floor of my closet, just waiting for me to trip over them.

Is there such a thing as having too many pairs of shoes? I would like to say, "No! You can never have too much of a good thing, right?" But you and I know this is not true. Too much candy will make your stomach hurt and, well, too many shoes will make your closet a mess!

Having too much of something or taking more than what you need is called *greed*. Did you know that when you are greedy, it could mean that you don't trust God to give you what you need?

This happened to the Israelites in the Bible. God gave the Israelites manna while they were wandering in the desert. Manna was a miracle food from God. God told the people to only take what they needed and to not keep it overnight. He promised to give them more each day. He wanted to teach the Israelites to trust Him. But some of the Israelites did not listen and they took too much. They were being greedy! But the extra manna became rotten with worms and started to stink. They ended up wasting a lot of the delicious food that God had given them because they did not trust Him to give them all that they needed.

Can you think of something that you need and love but that you may have too much of? Maybe it is shoes or toys. Maybe, like the Israelites, you take too many cookies or too much ice cream. God wants you to share what you have and trust Him to provide what you need. He does not want you to depend on anything but Him.

Practice not taking more than you need and trusting God to give you the things you need, when you need them.

Dear God, I have been greedy in the past. Please help me know when I'm not trusting You and self-ishly trying to keep as much of something as I can. Thank You for providing everything I need exactly when I need it. In Jesus's name, amen.

Every Day Is a Good Day

Some days just start off wrong. You know the mornings where you can't find your favorite jeans? Or the day all of your socks are dirty? Or when your hair just won't "do right," and then you find out there is no milk for your cereal...after you have poured it into your bowl!

There is no question about it: These days are hard. You may just want to cry, scream, slam a door, and lock yourself in your room for the rest of the day!

But you can't! Your family would not want you to do that, it would not make you feel any better, and most importantly, God does not want you to behave that way!

James 1:2-4 reminds us to "Consider it pure joy...whenever you face trials of many kinds, because you know that the testing of your faith produces perseverance. Let perseverance finish its work so that you may be mature and complete, not lacking anything."

Yes, you read that right! God says that challenges and tests (including difficult mornings) are to be treated like a gift! Sounds weird, right?

God is not saying that He is happy that you are having a bad day. He's not telling you to pretend to be happy about it either. Instead, He just wants you to think about it differently. He wants you to use those days to show what you know about Him and the difference He makes in your life!

It is pretty easy to be loving, peaceful, joyful, and all smiles when things are going great. But difficult mornings, hard days, and even hard weeks are the perfect way to practice showing your godly character—Jesus in you.

So next time things are not going your way, do not lock yourself in your room! Instead, ask God what He is trying to teach you and how you can grow from what is happening.

Dear God, this is a really hard lesson to learn. When bad things happen or things just don't go my way, please help me to focus on You and to find joy even as I walk in not-so-fun moments and days. Help me to remember that You are growing me when these things happen! In Jesus's name, amen.

A Little Brave

Have you ever seen a little boy or girl dressed as their favorite superhero? There is something about wearing a cape that makes them feel so powerful! They jump around swinging swords and saying things like, "To the rescue" or "Up, up, up and away!" While they are wearing the costume, they feel like they can do anything and beat anyone.

Whenever I see a little kid pretending to be fearless and brave, I think of the story of David and Goliath. I have never heard of anyone braver than David, and he was not pretending!

David was a young boy—the baby in his family. David's people, the Israelites, were being tortured and bullied by the Philistines. Every day a giant bully named Goliath would come close to where David lived and ask someone to come and fight him. Of course no one ever wanted to fight him because of how big and scary he was!

David decided he wanted to fight, and he volunteered to go. Everyone thought David was crazy because he decided not to take any of the weapons people thought he would need to win. But do you know what? David was brave because he knew he had special powers. Not from wearing a cape or carrying a sword, but from God! David said in 1 Samuel 17:47, "All those gathered here will know that it is not by sword or spear that the LORD saves; for the battle is the LORD's, and he will give all of you into our hands."

And guess what? David was right! With just a few rocks that God told him to take, David beat the big giant! David was not brave because he worked so hard or because he was so strong. David was brave because he trusted in God.

Are you facing something you need to be brave for? It may be a person, a test, or just a hard situation. Be like David. Ask God what He wants you to do. God gave David just what he needed to beat a giant, and He will do the same thing for you. So remember that you don't need a cape or special powers to feel brave. You have God!

Dear God, sometimes I'm afraid to face what is ahead. Please help me face whatever comes my way. I know You have given me power to face any giant as long as I depend on You. In Jesus's name, amen.

Be Careful—
It's Contagious

To imitate someone means that you copy what they do, what they say, or how they behave. Sometimes you may choose to imitate something because you like it and it seems like a cool thing to do. But sometimes you may be imitating someone or something and not even realize you are doing it.

For example, my third-grade teacher would use two fingers to squeeze her nose when she sneezed. Her sneezes had the cutest sound ever! It would also help her to avoid the embarrassment of a fly away or leaky sneeze. I thought this was a brilliant idea and without even realizing it, I began to do it myself. I still do it today.

It's almost like some things are just contagious and if you spend enough time around it you just cannot help but to "catch" it. Has this ever happened to you? It is totally normal to "catch" certain actions from your friends or family members because you are always around them. But do you realize that you can also "catch" certain behaviors, words, and attitudes from people on a television show or in a magazine or book that you read?

God wants you to pay special attention to who and what you imitate, which means that you also need to be careful about who you are around the most and what you spend a lot of time doing. You have to be careful not to "catch" or copy things that are not like Jesus!

In 3 John 11 we are told, "Do not imitate what is evil but what is good. Anyone who does what is good is from God. Anyone who does what is evil has not seen God."

Dear God, help me know when I catch the wrong attitude or the wrong way of reacting when things do not go my way. And help me to spend so much time with You and people who love You that I catch a bit more of You each day. In Jesus's name, amen.

Think about the way you spend your time and answer the following questions.

Do you enjoy...

Watching TV?

What is your favorite show or movie?

What do you like about it? Is it funny or adventurous?

What type of things do the characters do?

Hanging out with friends?

What do you like to do with them?

What do you talk about most?

Are your friends kind and generous to others?

Reading books?

What is your favorite book?

Who are the characters?

How do they behave? Are they kind, rude, smart, obedient?

Now, think back over your answers. Are you spending more time filling your heart and mind with things God wants for you or things He does not want for you? What actions and attitudes are you copying from a television show, a friend, or a book, maybe without even realizing it? If the behavior you're copying isn't godly, then it is probably time to make some changes!

Just a Drop

Pretend there is a glass of water on the table and you add a tiny drop of green liquid food coloring. What do you think will happen?

If you said the water will turn green, you are correct!

Now pretend you had the same glass of water and the same amount of food coloring, but you only want to make half the water green. Can you?

If you said no, then you are correct again!

There is no way to add food coloring to just a little bit of a glass of water. Once you pour the drop of green in, you will change the way the entire glass looks. The only way to remove the green is to dump it out and fill up the glass with clear, fresh water.

The thoughts that enter your mind are just like the little drops of food coloring that enter a glass of water. "Drops" of negative thoughts will eventually come out in the way you talk, the way you feel, and the way you treat others. Positive thoughts will do the same. You are the only one who can control what drops you pour in!

God wants you to choose to fill your heart and mind with drops of Him and His love. Philippians 4:8 says, "Whatever is true, whatever is noble, whatever is right, whatever is pure, whatever is lovely, whatever is admirable—if anything is excellent or praiseworthy—think about such things."

There will always be negative things for you to think about. But you can choose to fill your mind with God's love by looking for Him in the things around you at all times! For example, on a rainy day choose to thank God for sending food for the trees and the grass. Or when your teacher gives you too much homework, don't complain about how hard it is. Instead thank God for the brain He has given you to be able to learn! Today, watch what type of drops you pour into your glass!

Dear God, help me to fill my mind and heart with Your love and the things that will make me more like You. Please get rid of anything negative that might make me less like You. In Jesus's name, amen.

How to Pray

Has someone ever asked you to pray out loud and you were so afraid that you felt like all of your words left your brain and your mouth was empty? Or maybe you have been in your room alone trying to pray and after you begin with, "Dear God," you just have no idea what you should say next?

Don't worry. It happens to all of us!

When I was a little girl I remember sitting in church, watching and listening to the people around me as they worshipped God. And when they prayed they knew exactly what to say. Their words were really big and they seemed perfect. I remember thinking to myself, "I can't do that. I don't even know what those words mean!"

Prayer is simply your special conversation with God. And God wants you to have conversations with Him all the time! You may think you only know small words or that your sentences don't make much sense, but God is not looking for fancy prayers. He wants you to pray from your heart.

Colossians 4:2 says, "Devote yourselves to prayer, being watchful and thankful." This means that God wants you to talk to Him about everything—anytime you want. You can talk to Him about your homework, your favorite foods, a fight you had with a friend, or even the weather!

There are no set rules or plans for how you need to talk to God. Just open your heart and share what's inside. You can thank Him for loving you, ask Him for anything you need, and pray for others. There is nothing too big or too small to ask Him for, or too serious, sad, or silly to share with Him. You will never get on His nerves and He will always hear you.

Take time to pray today. When you pray from your heart you cannot go wrong!

Writing your prayers helps you to share what is inside your heart. If you keep the prayers you write, you can read them later to see how God has answered them or if He has changed your heart!

Make a prayer box to store your written prayers! You will need:

- 1 box, any color or size
- scrapbook paper sheets (different colors and patterns)
- embellishments, ribbon, trim (optional)
- glue
- small container of Mod Podge®
- foam brush
- scissors
- newspaper

Step One:

Cover your work area with newspaper because you do not want to ruin your kitchen table!

Step Two:

Cut or rip your scrapbook sheets into pieces. Make sure there are a variety of different shapes, sizes, and patterns, enough to cover the outside of the box and the lid.

Step Three:

Choose a piece of paper and glue it onto the box.

Step Four:

Continue adding pieces of paper until the entire box is covered. Make sure the paper overlaps so that none of the box is showing.

Step Five:

When all four sides have been covered with the decorated paper, brush extra Mod Podge over the entire box to seal it and make it shiny! Let your box dry 20 minutes before gluing on letters, ribbons, buttons, or gems.

A Good Job

Making up a new game or playing pretend with friends is a great way to use your imagination. You can create new things to do and make-believe places to live. You can be an astronaut, a doctor, an Olympic champion, or a mommy—and the best part is, you can even pretend you are all of these things in one single game. The possibilities really are limitless!

You may not realize it, but playing pretend is also a fun way to practice or prepare for a job or something important you have to do in your real life.

Think about it this way. The way really good athletes, singers, and actors prepare for a big game or show is by pretending to do it before the big day. This is called *practice* or *rehearsal*. When athletes practice, they are pretending to be in the middle of a real game. Actors recite their lines and singers rehearse the words to their songs.

A game of pretend or a practice can be good for a lot of reasons! You may not have a big game that you are getting ready for, but God has given you a job. The Bible says in 2 Corinthians 5:20 that you are an ambassador for Christ. *Ambassador* may sound like a really big word, but it is just a person who represents someone else. This means that once you accept Jesus Christ into your life, God gives you the job of showing His love to others.

Showing Jesus's love is not hard because it's the way you live all the time. But you do have to be prepared. Here is one way you can practice. When you are pretending to be an astronaut, a doctor, or a mommy, make sure you are practicing being one who shows Jesus with her words, attitudes, and actions! Yup, this means you can practice being an ambassador for Christ even while you are playing with your friends!

How else can you practice your job?

Dear God, thank You for giving me a relationship with You through Jesus. Help me to always practice sharing Your love and message of Jesus with others so they will know You too. In Jesus's name, amen.

You want to be the best ambassador for Christ that you can be, don't you? So let's practice! Write your answers to the questions below and practice what you can say to others about who Jesus is.

1. Who is Jesus?

_____

_____

_____

2. Why do you love Him?

_____

_____

_____

3. Why do people need to know about God?

_____

_____

_____

You can even turn it into a fun game with a friend! Take turns and practice sharing what Jesus means to you and why you love Him so much.

The Problem with Spinach

Has anything embarrassing ever happened to you?

One of the most embarrassing things that has ever happened to me is when I looked in the mirror at the end of the day and I saw a piece of green spinach sitting in between my two front teeth. The last time it happened (yes, it has happened more than once!) was hours after dinner, so I spent that night thinking about all of the different people I had talked to. I am sure they all saw the green spinach but no one told me it was there!

Has this ever happened to you, or have you ever seen this happen to someone? Were you the one to tell your friend the food was there, or did you watch her talk and think, *Gross!* without ever saying a word?

Sometimes friends have to tell each other hard and embarrassing things in order to help them out. God tells us to! Proverbs 27:6 says, "Wounds from a friend can be trusted." This means that when someone loves you, you can trust that what they are telling you is true, even if it hurts. Friends should never just say mean things to try to be hurtful, but if you see a friend making a bad decision or falling into a bad situation, you should try to help them out!

Ask God to give you friends you can be honest with and who will be honest with you, even when it hurts. God wants you to always try to point your friends to see His truth and help keep them from falling. Friends who point each other toward Jesus are the best friends!

Are you that kind of friend? Do you have friends that will speak truth with you?

Dear God, thank You for being a friend who always speaks truth to me in Your Word. Help me to be a friend who speaks truth and help me to keep close friendships with people who will speak truth to me, even when it hurts. In Jesus's name, amen.

Who Are You Working For?

Awards are awesome! They really look great hanging on a bedroom wall or sitting on a shelf. If you have ever won an award, you should be very proud. After practicing and working hard toward something, a shiny trophy, a certificate trimmed in gold with your name on it, or even a few encouraging words are a great way for others to see and celebrate your efforts. It always feels good to have someone notice your hard work.

But even if no one ever notices the good things that you do, you should still keep doing your best. The kind of heart you have on the inside matters more than the number of trophies you have. Your heart is way more important than the work you do that others can see. God sees your heart and promises to reward you for it!

Colossians 3:23-24 says, "Whatever you do, work at it with all your heart, as working for the Lord, not for human masters, since you know that you will receive an inheritance from the Lord as a reward. It is the Lord Christ you are serving." God wants you to remember that while awards and being noticed are nice, what matters most is the kind of heart you have. Your teachers and your coaches cannot see your heart, only God can. Your teacher may give you a certificate for having perfect attendance, but God wants to make sure that when you are at school, you are kind to others, you are a good listener, you make good decisions, and that you let your friends see His love.

Work hard and do your best, but always remember who you are really working for. When you work for God and have a heart to please Him, you will get the best reward. He promises to give you eternal rewards in heaven as you live with Him forever.

Dear God, I know You care about my heart. Help me to remember that I work for You. When I am doing something I love, or even when I am doing something I don't enjoy, help me remember that You see what is happening on the inside! In Jesus's name, amen.

God Made Them Too

Being a girl is awesome! You can wear big fluffy hair bows or one bouncy ponytail, sparkly nail polish or none at all, sneakers, sandals or cowgirl boots, jeans or dresses. As a girl you can be and do anything because God took His time and made you just the way He wanted you. He made you special.

But do you know something else? God made boys too! Talking about boys may gross you out or make you giggle, but you should remember that boys are God's special creation too.

Yes, being a boy is a lot different from being a girl. Sometimes boys enjoy different games, they look different, and they can certainly smell different. God did make boys and girls different, but He still made both to be just like Him!

Genesis 1:27 says, "So God created mankind in his own image, in the image of God he created them; male and female he created them."

To be made in God's image means that we have His heart and as His boys and girls, we should do our best to act like Him. So when you are talking to boys in your class or even to your brothers at home, remember that they are God's boys. It is important to love them, be kind to them, and always point them to God. Both boys and girls are fearfully and wonderfully made and God cares about us all!

Dear God, thank You for making me to be like You. Can You help me remember that You made boys in Your image too? I'm so thankful that we can know You and become more like You as we get to know You more. In Jesus's name, amen.

Seek and Find

At this time in your life it is perfectly normal to like boys a little, but to mostly think they are pretty gross. One day you will probably start to like boys a little more and start to see them as a little less gross. You might wonder what it would be like to have a boyfriend—or even a husband someday.

There is nothing wrong with seeking God about the type of future He wants you to have. That may include talking to Him about the boy who will become your husband. But for now, the best thing you can do is to begin to talk to God about what He wants for you as you get older.

There are many special days ahead for you, and the Bible tells you exactly what you can do to prepare for them. Matthew 6:33 says, "Seek first his kingdom and his righteousness, and all these things will be given to you as well." This means that no matter what anyone else is doing, the best thing you can do is focus your attention on finding out all you can about God and praying for those around you. Seeking God means to talk to Him about everything you do and every decision you have to make.

Will you seek God today for your future?

Dear God, my mind wanders in so many directions and there are so many things that I want to do, see, and have. Help me look for You and put You first in everything I do. In Jesus's name, amen.

Fear God, But Do Not Be Afraid

What do you think of God? Do you think about what He looks like? Do you ever think about how He acts? Do you ever imagine Him smiling and laughing with you? Maybe you have heard someone say that you should "fear God," and that made you think God is mean and scary.

God does want you to fear Him, but not in a scary way. He wants you to respect Him, like you would a teacher, a coach, or a police officer. Police officers are around to protect you. Teachers and coaches are around to teach you what they know and to help you make good decisions. When they are in the room, you act differently and make sure you are on your best behavior. You listen to them and you do what they say. Right?

This is what God expects from you too. He knows what is best for you. Just like that police officer, He wants you to be safe not only for yourself but for those around you. Like that teacher, He wants to teach you what He knows. And like that coach, He wants to train you and make you into a superstar for His team.

Psalm 112:1 says, "Blessed are those who fear the LORD, who find great delight in his commands." Fearing God means that you are happy to obey Him because you believe He knows what is best for you.

Don't ever be too afraid to talk to God when you do something wrong or to ask Him for help when you need it. Always remember that God sees you, knows you, and wants to help you! You can't do anything to make God love you more, but cheerfully obeying Him does bring you closer to Him.

Dear God, help me understand what it means to fear You. I do not want to be afraid of You, but I want to respect You. Thank You for teaching me and taking care of me. In Jesus's name, amen.

His Love Never Changes

When I was your age, I worked really hard for months to collect and save dimes to send to missionaries in Guatemala. I saved so much that my church gave me an award!

The pastor sat all of us kids on the stage and called our names, one by one, to shake his hand and get our certificate. When it was my turn, the congregation clapped very loud...well, it was mostly my mother because she was so proud of me! I was proud of myself too, and even more than that, I felt like God was the proudest He had ever been.

Before this, I had done quite a few things that I knew didn't make Him proud. Like the time I decided to draw big red check marks all around our living room walls. Or the time I screamed, "I HATE YOU!" so loudly at my brother that he ran out of the room and cried.

Yup, I had a pretty long list of not-so-proud moments. No matter how hard I tried, I could never seem to do the right thing all of the time. But on that day, on that stage, I knew I had done my best and it felt great!

The only problem was that I did not realize God loved me the same whether I was standing on the stage accepting an award or buried shamefully under the pillows on my bed. I didn't know that even when I messed up, God still loved me.

Maybe you have a list of not-so-great behaviors and wonder if God could still love you. The answer is yes! He will never stop loving you. You can never do enough good things to make Him love you more. And you can never do enough bad things to make Him love you less.

Romans 8:38-39 says, "I am convinced that neither death nor life, neither angels nor demons, neither the present nor the future, nor any powers, neither height nor depth, nor anything else in all creation, will be able to separate us from the love of God that is in Christ Jesus our Lord." This means that your behavior has nothing to do with God's love for you. His love does not grow and it certainly does not shrink! His love is like the ocean—big and deep, and reaching further than your eyes can see, every single day of every single year. Always remember that you are loved by the creator of the world and no matter what you do, you can't make Him change His mind about that!

Dear God, thank You for loving me no matter what! Help me to remember that Your love never changes. Will You help me love others the way You love me? In Jesus's name, amen.

Hide It

When it comes to the Bible, memorizing Scripture is the easy part.

Think about it. When you are just memorizing something, you don't even have to understand what it means. All you have to do is choose a verse or two, read it, and repeat it until the words become planted in your brain just long enough for you to say them out loud *without looking*.

God wants you to be able to do much more than repeat words from the Bible. He wants you to learn how to live what the Bible teaches you.

Psalm 119:11 says, "I have hidden your word in my heart that I might not sin against you." The key to understanding what the Bible says is hiding the words in your heart. When you hide something, you put it away in a safe place to protect it. You remember where you put it and you keep it close! This is what God wants you to do with the Bible. He doesn't want you to just memorize a scripture and then forget about it. He wants you to hide it close in your heart so you can pull it out when you need to. Knowing God's Word will help you when you face a challenge, when you feel lonely or afraid, or when you just want to be close to Him.

You may already have lots of verses memorized, and that is great! Now, take it a little further and begin to hide them in your heart.

Dear God, thank You for Your words in the Bible. Help me to understand them and hide them deep in my heart so I can live by them. In Jesus's name, amen.

Here are a few tips to help make sure you are hiding God's Word in your heart!

1. Choose a scripture you want to hide.
2. Write it on a piece of paper. You can even make it an art project and decorate a poster or card!
3. Place it in a place where you will see it often.
4. Pray and ask God to teach you what it means. If you need to, ask an adult to help explain it to you.
5. Rewrite it in your own words.
6. Think about the scripture often and always look for ways to use it in your actions.

Full of Truth

ruth. I know you have heard that word before. I am sure that if I asked you to use it in a sentence you probably could, right? But what if I asked you to tell me what the word *truth* means? Could you?

Everything you will ever need to know about the truth is already written for you in one book—the Bible. The truth is what God says about any and everything. And every single page of the Bible has truth written all over it.

Sometimes it's easier to believe something simply because someone else *said* it was true or you *feel* that it's true. But how can you really know?

You have to read God's Word. It is that simple. It does not matter what your friends say or what you see others doing. It does not matter how you feel and it really doesn't even matter if you like it. If God says it, it's the truth and it is good for you!

Second Timothy 3:16-17 tells us that "All Scripture is God-breathed and is useful for teaching, rebuking, correcting and training in righteousness, so that the servant of God may be thoroughly equipped for every good work." The Bible will help you grow up in your relationship with God and it will teach you. It will also tell you when you are wrong and help you make it right.

With Jesus and His truth inside of us, we are made whole and ready to do anything and everything that He is calling us to do! As you continue to grow as a young lady, your decisions will become more and more important. God wants you to know the truth so that you can live your life in a way that pleases Him and is best for you. Look for truth today!

Dear God, I want to know what You think about everything. I want to know how to live for You. Will You show me things in my life that may be wrong and help me make them right? Help me believe what You say and tell others about Your truth. In Jesus's name, amen.

Getting to Know Him

There is no way for us to know what God looks like, but it is important to remember that He is not just a big idea without a face. God has a heart and He wants you to get to know Him. The more you know about God's character the better your relationship can be.

When you hang out with your friends and get to know them, you begin to talk like them and act like them. It is the same with God. Spending time with Him will make you more like Jesus in how you think and how you act!

Read a few scriptures that help you learn more about who God really is!

God is love (1 John 4:8). He not only loves you, but love is who He is! That means that God cannot do anything mean or hateful. Yes, God can be disappointed and even angry when people do not choose to love Him, but even then His disappointment is because His love is so big that He wants everyone to have it. Every thought He has and every action He does is in love. No one can love like Him, but if you know Him, then His love is in you!

God is patient (2 Peter 3:9). God waits for you to receive Him, He forgives you every time you ask, and He never rushes you! God takes His time to make sure everyone has a chance to know His love!

God is creative (Genesis 1:1). Think about

the world and all of the details in it. From the shape of a star to every single different type of tree and animal right down to the texture of your hair, God designed it all!

God is smart (Psalm 33:13-15). Okay, actually God is more than just smart. He knows everything about everything and everybody...because He made it all!

And best of all...*God never ever changes* (Hebrews 13:8). Everything that is true about who God is today will always be true! You don't have to worry that one day He may be in a bad mood or may stop loving you. You can relax knowing that He does not change!

Dear God, thank You for helping me get to know You! Help me to remember that You are love, You are smart, You are patient, and You are creative. Thank You for making me like You. And can You help me be even more like You? In Jesus's name, amen.

Adopted

Do you know what it means to be adopted? Maybe you have a friend that has been adopted or maybe you are even adopted yourself!

Adoption is really special. When someone is adopted they are selected to be a part of a new family. That person now has loving parents and possibly even new brothers and sisters. They even have new grandparents, aunts, uncles, and cousins.

You see, being adopted changes everything. A person who is adopted goes from having no family to having a huge family and all the love and benefits that come with it. When you are adopted it is as if you were always a part of the new family that you have joined.

If you are God's child then you have been adopted too! The Bible tells us that when we trust Jesus as our Savior, He adopts us into His family. God becomes our Father and we become His child. And just like being adopted into a family, as a child of God, you get new brothers and sisters. Remember, He has other children just like you!

Ephesians 1:5 says that God "predestined us for adoption to sonship through Jesus Christ, in accordance with his pleasure and will." God wants you to celebrate with Him that you are a part of His family. When families adopt children it makes them really happy to bring a new child into their home, and

God is no different. Remember, He invented adoption and put it in our hearts!

If you have nothing else to celebrate today, remember that you can always celebrate God making you His child!

Dear God, thank You for sending Jesus so I could become a part of Your family. I feel so special and grateful that You chose to adopt me. Never let me forget that I am Your child! Help me celebrate and show others how great it is to be a part of Your family. In Jesus's name, amen.

Doubt

Doubt is the feeling you have when you are unsure about something or when you do not trust that something is true. There are many different reasons why you have doubts. For example, you may doubt that you will pass a test because you know that you did not study hard. Well, if you didn't study, then you probably should have a bit of concern! But maybe you doubt you will pass because you just think it's too hard for you to learn. You and I both know that if you study and do your homework, then passing should not even be a question. In this case, your doubt is untrue and makes no sense at all!

There will be times when you doubt and do not believe a teacher, a friend, or even God, and you may be really confused with what to do about it. Understanding your feelings of doubt can be tricky, and the key to getting rid of doubt is learning the truth.

There are several stories of people who experienced doubt in the Bible, and God always points them to the truth. One example is John the Baptist. In the book of Matthew, God sent John the Baptist to help prepare the hearts of people Jesus would talk to. John the Baptist ended up in jail for talking about Jesus. While he was there he really began to doubt that Jesus was the actual Son of God. He asked Jesus, "Are you the one who is to come, or should we expect someone else?" (Matthew 11:3).

When Jesus heard this, He got John the Baptist to stop doubting by reminding him of things he already knew to be true. Jesus had healed people and performed a lot of miracles that no one else could do. Once John the Baptist remembered these things, all of his doubt had to leave! He knew what was true.

When you experience doubt, be like John the Baptist and use it as a chance to search for and remember the truth! Do not just accept that what you feel is true. Instead pray that God helps you to find the real answer. Doubting is not good for you and it is not what God wants for you. He wants you to "[walk] in the truth" (3 John 4).

Dear God, I'm so glad Your Word is true. Thank You that I can trade my doubt for what You have to say about everything and anything. In Jesus's name, amen.

Worth Waiting For

Have you ever wanted something even though you knew it was not good for you? Sometimes you have to choose between waiting for the best and settling for something that feels good right now. There is a story like this in the Bible! Maybe it will help to explain what I mean.

In Genesis 25 you can read the story of twin brothers, Jacob and Esau. Esau was the oldest, and because he was the oldest he had been promised a birthright. A birthright was what a father would pass down to his oldest son. It was very special. He did not have to work for it or earn it. These special promises were his just because he was born first. All he had to do was wait until the time was right.

Esau did not want to wait.

One day he had been out hunting and was very hungry. He walked into the house and asked his brother, Jacob, for something to eat. Jacob said he would give Esau something to eat right then, but he wanted Esau to give him his birthright in return. Sadly, Esau traded his birthright for some food. He got what he wanted but lost something very special.

It may not be a piece of candy or a bowl of soup, but just like Esau, there will always be something that looks better, feels better, or tastes better right now. Think about your life. What choices are you making because they feel good right now but are not good for you later?

Isaiah 26:8 says, "Yes, LORD, walking in the way of your laws, we wait for you; your name and renown are the desire of our hearts." You may think waiting for something is hard, and it can be! But God promises to give you the strength to do it.

Dear God, sometimes I get impatient and would rather have what I want instead of waiting for what You or my parents have for me. Please make me strong as I choose to wait. In Jesus's name, amen.

A Not-So-Funny Joke

Why did the spider have a hard time finding food on the computer?

The answer is at the bottom of the page. Before you look at it, let's talk about jokes. Don't you love a good one? I sure do! Laughter is a great way to make others feel good. If you are ever around a group of quiet or sleepy people, tell a joke. It is a sure way to wake the crowd up! It also feels good to be the "funny girl." Being funny can make you the popular one. The girl everyone wants to be around and sit next to. Laughter means happy, and people like to feel happy.

However, sometimes jokes and laughter can make a person feel bad.

You know the jokes that make fun of other people or tease them? Even though some people may think it's funny, it really doesn't feel good for the person everyone is laughing at. It is important to be mindful of the things you say about people, even if you and others are having fun. If someone's feelings are hurt or they are sad because of things you are saying, you need to stop and apologize.

Do not ever let being funny for some people make you mean or rude to others. In the same way your jokes can wake up a crowd, they can destroy a person. God wants you to use your words to

Because he didn't search the web!

encourage others, not make them feel bad. Words are powerful. Proverbs 18:21 tells us that "The tongue has the power of life and death." Pray that God helps you to know the difference between a funny joke and a mean one!

Dear God, I pray that You would help me not to hurt others with my words, even if I think they are funny. Help me know the difference between being funny and being mean. In Jesus's name, amen.

Love to Love

When you think of love, do you think of smiley faces, twinkly eyes, lots of laughing, and happy conversations?

Love is super easy and fun when the people that you love are kind and generous. But what about people who are not really that kind? Do you love them? Do you have to?

The answer is *yes*. God wants you to love everyone, not just the people who are nice to you and love you back. This means that you should love the girl in school who makes unkind comments and gives you mean looks. You should also love the teacher who mistreats you. You should even love people you don't know. God wants you to love them all. After all, every person on this earth is His precious creation.

God's love is different from others'. It's the kind of love no one deserves. Nice people don't deserve it and neither do mean people, but He still gives it out to everyone! You can't earn God's love by behaving a certain way or doing certain things. He loves you just because He does.

If you don't have to earn God's love, then should other people have to earn yours? In John 13:34-35 Jesus says, "A new command I give you: Love one another. As I have loved you, so you must love one another. By this everyone will know that you are my disciples, if you love one another."

God's love is for everyone. His love changes people. It makes sad moments feel better and it teaches you how to make wrong things right. Everyone needs to know this type of love. Decide to love everyone today and ask God for the strength that it will take!

Dear God, thank You for loving me. Will You help me show others Your love today? Help me love everyone because You do! In Jesus's name, amen.

Dreams

Will you dream with me for a minute? Not like a sleepy dream, but more of a daydream. So you have to stay awake, okay? Think about what you want your life to be like when you get older. Do you have job? A house? A husband? How many children? What color is the front door to your house? What color are the walls? Where do you work? Do you have good friends?

Keep dreaming for as long as you want. It is really fun to picture every detail of your life, and you may even want to write your dreams down to keep them fresh in your mind!

Now, of course you have no way of really making all the things in your dream come true, but it is good to have a vision or a goal for your life. There are always things you can do, even now, to make sure you are headed in the right direction. Some things are good to do no matter what dreams you have, like studying hard and doing your best in school.

But there are also things you can start doing that are more specific to the goals you have in mind. For example, if your dream is to become a doctor, then why not start volunteering at a nursing home? You can read to the patients or take them treats. You may not be able to treat people with medicine, but you can surround yourself with doctors and nurses who know what they are doing, and you can treat people with kindness while you observe. If you want to be a singer or an actress, then you can look for places to practice and audition, like school, church plays, and programs.

As you dream, begin to ask yourself what one thing you can do today to get one step closer to your dream. Before you know it you might just be living your dream! Dreams don't always come true, but they certainly won't if you don't make decisions to follow them.

In Psalm 119:133 we read a prayer that you can pray too: "Direct my footsteps according to your word." Pray and ask God to help you to have a goal for your life, and make sure you ask Him to guide you in what you do!

Dear God, thank You for giving me such a great imagination to think and dream about what my future could look like. Please give me wisdom as I try to walk toward the plans You have for me. Most of all, direct my steps. In Jesus's name, amen.

Already Down

Mariah tripped and fell into a huge puddle of dirty brown water. The muddy water splashed all over her face, and her outfit was ruined! Just as Mariah was getting up, her classmate Tina walked over and pushed her back into the puddle. Tina then ran off to join her friends. Mariah could not believe that Tina would be so mean! She slouched down deeper into the puddle and cried.

If you were to see this happen you would probably think that Tina was the meanest person ever, wouldn't you? How could she push her classmate back into the mud instead of helping her get up?

It may be hard to imagine, but this actually happens a lot. Think about it this way. It may not be muddy water, but have you felt a little happy when someone gets in trouble for something they did to you? Maybe your sister hit you and while she was being punished for it, you smiled. And then after her punishment, you walked by her and joyfully said, "Told you!"

Delighting or rejoicing in someone else's failure is never the right thing to do. It's just like pushing them in the mud. And the Bible tells us not to do it. Proverbs 24:17 says, "Do not gloat when your enemy falls; when they stumble, do not let your heart rejoice." The next time you see someone having a bad day or being punished for a mistake, ask God to show you ways to encourage them. Be the one that picks them up out of the mud!

Dear God, help me to be an encourager—the person You depend on to pick other people up from the mud. Show me those who are hurting and give me the courage to be and show Your love. In Jesus's name, amen.

How You Wear It

Is fashion important to you? Having just the right pair of jeans and the coolest pair of sneakers may matter a lot, but instead of focusing on what you are wearing, make sure you really think about how you wear it.

Is that totally confusing? Let me explain. The color of your favorite skirt is not important. But the length of it matters a lot! Whether your shirt has stripes, buttons, polka dots, or flowers is totally up to you and your style. You can layer and match (or mismatch!) whatever you want. But when you put it on, pay attention to how it fits.

Being aware of how your clothes fit and look can be described as *modesty*. When it comes to your clothes, *modest* is sort of a fancy word for *appropriate* or *proper*. Sometimes you may be tempted to spend hours in front of the mirror trying to put together the perfect outfit. But when you are done, always use your mirror to make sure your outfit is modest.

You always want to make sure that your perfect outfit feels great to you and is appropriate for others to look at. There are no set rules to define what is modest and what is not. It's much more of a heart issue. Your body is such a special creation and God wants to make sure you always treat it like that!

First Corinthians 6:19-20 reminds us, "Do you not know that your bodies are temples of the Holy Spirit, who is in you, whom you have received from God? You are not your own; you were bought at a price. Therefore honor God with your bodies."

Pray and ask God to help you remember that your body is His and the way you wear your clothes matters!

Dear God, thank You for fashion and the style You have given me! Will You help me to honor You with the way I wear my clothes? In Jesus's name, amen.

Here are two tips to help you stay fashionably modest!

- Pick out a pair of cool leggings to wear under your shorts or a skirt. That way you can make sure no one gets an accidental peek under it.

- Shirts can be tricky because they move when you move. If you bend over the front can go down and if you raise your arms up high...well, your shirt does too! Layering your shirts will fix this. A longer shirt underneath will help to make sure the front is not too low and the back is not too short.

Jesus Came

Does the Bible ever totally confuse you? It's okay to be honest! Sometimes the Bible can be a little hard to understand. The Old Testament has stories of people fighting each other, animals being sacrificed, and even God destroying nations. But then when you get to the New Testament the sacrifices seem to stop (except one, but we will get to that soon!), God does not destroy any more nations, and everyone seems to be fighting over whether or not they believe that Jesus is God's Son.

Want to know what happens and changes things between the Old and New Testament? Jesus. His life changes everything. He changed everything then, and He changes everything now! Jesus changes you and me and our relationship with God.

In the Old Testament, people had to sacrifice animals to pay for their sins. However, the Bible tells us that God sent Jesus to be the perfect payment, which means that people no longer have to sacrifice animals. Now, Jesus's perfect love makes everything right between God and His people. No animal or action could ever be good enough to make us right with God, so He sent Jesus to take care of it.

Do you know how wonderful this news is? It means that you do not have to keep working to be good enough for God. God does not need you to prove how good you are. He wants you to have the unconditional love that He sent in His Son, Jesus.

Titus 3:5 says, "He saved us, not because of righteous things we had done, but because of his mercy. He saved us through the washing of rebirth and renewal by the Holy Spirit." God showed how much He loves you by sending Jesus to die for your sins. Now, He wants you to accept that love and allow Him to make you clean.

Dear God, thank You for paying for my sins and making me right with You. Thank You for the reminder that I am made right and good because of You. Help me to never try to earn Your love, but to rest knowing that You love me already. Thank You for the changes You make in my life and in the world! In Jesus's name, amen.

Yummy Honey

Have you ever seen a honeycomb? They pretty much look like a bunch of tiny tunnels shaped like hexagons (a shape with six sides) that are all stuck together. Honeybees build these honeycombs inside their nests.

Now, what do you think each tunnel is full of? Yup, you guessed it! A honeycomb is full of young bees...and honey! Honey is a delicious, sticky substance that bees make. It is good to eat, and it is used for many great things. For example, because of its sweet taste, you can use it instead of sugar in your tea or mix it with your peanut butter instead of jelly! Honey is also great when you don't feel good. If you have a sore throat or a bad cough, you can swallow a spoonful of honey to help. Because honey is thick and sticky, it helps to cover your throat and protects it while it gets better.

I do not think that it is an accident that the Bible tells us that pleasant words are like honeycombs! Proverbs 16:24 says, "Gracious words are a honeycomb, sweet to the soul and healing to the bones." Like a honeycomb, you are full of a helpful, sweet, and useful substance: your words! The words you use have the power to make others feel better when they are pleasant and good. When you use unpleasant words, well, you are doing the opposite. Unpleasant words are harmful and hurtful.

God wants you to use your words to protect others and not harm them. When you think of your words like honey, you have no choice but to make them sweet and yummy!

Dear God, help my words to be sweet like honey so that they will be helpful and healing to someone else today. In Jesus's name, amen.

Make a "Honey List!" This is a list of sweet words you can use. Try to look over your "honey list" every day and add to it. Keeping these words in the front of your brain will help you use them more often!

Praise

I am not really a big fan of sports. I would much rather curl up on the couch with a big cup of hot chocolate and read a book! However, every once in a while I do enjoy watching a good game of basketball or soccer, especially when it is a championship game. Championship games are a lot of fun to watch because the players want to win first place really, really bad, and wanting to win makes them play very hard. Everyone does their best, and even the fans scream and cheer hard for their favorite teams to win. Their cheers and excitement are how they encourage the players. Some fans scream so loud that they even lose their voices!

Have you ever done that? Screamed so loud for something or someone that you lost your voice? Whether you like sports or not, I am sure you can think of something that makes you so excited that you just cannot control yourself—jumping up and down, spinning in circles, or even crying.

That kind of excitement and energy is just what God wants you to have for Him! God wants you to be so excited for what He is doing in your life that you just have to celebrate. Showing your excitement and appreciation for God is called praise!

Hebrews 13:15 says, "Through Jesus...let us continually offer to God a sacrifice of praise—the fruit of lips that openly profess his name." The Bible tells us God loves it when His children praise Him. Praise is how we show God how grateful we are to Him and how excited we are about His love and what He is doing in our lives!

Just like fans at a sports game, everyone shows their excitement differently. You don't have to praise God the same way your friends do. The gratitude you have in your heart shows your excitement, and that can come out in a lot of different ways. It could be dancing. It could be singing. And you might not understand it, but for some it could be sitting quietly and thinking!

Praising God is personal. How you praise Him is a special part of your relationship with Him! How do you praise God? Do you have something to praise Him for today?

Dear God, thank You for giving me Jesus, who is the best reason to praise! Help me to remember each day to show You my thanks, no matter how it comes out. In Jesus's name, amen.

Anger

Y ou can't avoid getting angry sometimes. Everyone does. You might not think so, but the nicest person you know has been angry about something before. There are even stories in the Bible about Jesus getting angry—seriously!

One story in the Bible tells us that people were bringing children to meet Jesus. But the disciples were trying to send the children away, and this made Jesus very upset. The Bible says that Jesus became "indignant" and "rebuked" the disciples! (You can read the entire story for yourself in Mark 10:13-16). *Indignant* and *rebuked* are pretty big words that mean Jesus did not like what the disciples were doing.

Now, the Bible does not say that when Jesus became angry He screamed, stomped out of the room, and pushed people out of His way! How disappointing would it be if Jesus behaved that way? Instead, Jesus took time and talked to His disciples about what He was feeling. He was honest and told them how upset He was about what they were doing. He even explained why it made Him angry.

Yes, anger is an emotion you will feel sometimes. People will do things that you do not like and it may upset you. People can even be mean, but you can learn from Jesus. You can learn to handle your anger the right way. Ephesians 4:26 says, "In your anger do not sin: Do not let the sun go down while you are still angry." This means that even when you are angry, you can find the right way to handle it. You cannot be disrespectful and you certainly cannot use anger as a reason to treat someone mean!

Ask God to help you to be like Him even when you are angry!

Dear God, I sometimes get angry and in the past I have not made the best decisions in my anger. Please help me know how I can turn my anger into a way to serve You or someone else. Help me let anger go when it does not honor You. In Jesus's name, amen.

The next time you feel yourself getting angry, take a deep breath and count to three before you speak. This will give you time to really think about how you feel and what you really want to say.

Growing Up in God

I love babies! Do you? I love the way they smell, the wrinkles around their little ankles, and the way that they can curl their whole bodies up into a ball. I love when they start to smile at our faces! Soon after that they start learning to walk, and that is when the real fun begins!

Isn't it cool to think about how everyone starts off as a tiny baby and does not know anything? But as babies grow up they learn a whole lot in a very short time. As they get older, they are no longer happy to just stay wrapped up on someone's lap. Instead, they want to reach, smell, and touch everything they see. Something else happens too—the more they learn, the more people expect them to do what they have been taught. They have to use what they know in order to live.

When you were a baby, you did not understand that a stove is hot or that stairs can be dangerous. But when you got older, those things made more sense, right? Now, it would be a little weird for you to just walk up to a hot stove and touch it because you know that it will burn you. Now that you understand how a stove works, people expect you be careful around it.

This is also true when you grow in God. The more He teaches you, the more He wants you to use what you know. Just like babies, toddlers, and teenagers have parents or adults to help them, God gave His Word and the Holy Spirit to help you.

John 14:26 says that the Holy Spirit "will teach you all things and will remind you of everything I have said to you."

Reading your Bible and studying God's Word is a great way to learn and grow. But remember that you are not alone. The Holy Spirit will help you make good choices! God does not want you to stay a baby forever!

Dear God, thank You for sending the Holy Spirit to give me wise counsel and to remind me who I am in Jesus. Please teach me to listen to Your voice and help me to grow up in You! In Jesus's name, amen.

What Are You Thinking?

Emily turned around and thought, *I don't like you* as she walked into the kitchen to follow the directions her dad had given her. She stood at the sink alone and continued to think mean things about him as she washed the dishes. By the time she finished all of the dishes she was so angry! She even had tears in her eyes!

Emily knew that her parents could not know the terrible things she was thinking, so she was not worried about getting in trouble. However, she did not realize that her thoughts would make her feel horrible, and now she was even more upset than before. Even more than that, Emily did not realize that she needed to be careful with what she thinks in her head, because even if no one else knew, God did.

Do you know that even your thoughts matter?

I am sure you know that you should not say disrespectful things to an adult or mean things to a friend, right? But sometimes, you may think it is okay to say or think whatever you want when you are alone and no one is listening.

The Bible says that your thoughts matter and that your thoughts will control your actions and your life. Proverbs 4:23 reminds us, "Above all else, guard your heart, for everything you do flows from it." God wants you to keep your mind and your heart focused on Him, and that can't happen when your head is filled with negative and sinful thoughts!

Your mind is an open door to your heart. The words you think and say to yourself turn into feelings, and those feelings get inside your heart. Mean thoughts will pop into your head, but do not let them stay! Ask God to remove them and to help you keep your mind and heart clear of bad things! This way your mind can always be focused on Him.

Dear God, thank You for reminding me that my thoughts matter. Help me to know when bad thoughts start feeling at home in my mind, and help me replace those thoughts with ones that make You smile. In Jesus's name, amen.

Yellow Lines

Have you ever driven a car? Wait, don't answer that! Let's try again: Have you ever ridden in a car? Now that's more like it!

When you are riding in a car, you will notice yellow lines all over the roads. Some are dashed and some are very thick with no breaks. The lines are there to guide the cars and to keep them from bumping in to each other. Roads would be so confusing if those lines were not there! Can you imagine it? Cars would do whatever they wanted and there would be a lot of accidents. No one would know what they should do or how to stay safe while driving.

The lines on the road do not stop cars from going anywhere, but they do help people get where they are going safely. They are a guide, and they give the drivers boundaries. Yellow lines help drivers know which parts of the road they are supposed to use.

You may not be able to drive a car, but boundaries are very important for you too! The Bible is full of yellow lines and guidelines for your life. God wants to protect you, and following His advice and plans will keep you safe and get you where He wants you to be. His guide, the Bible, is here to help you steer and protect you! God does not want you to crash.

If you want to stay in the lines, you need

God's help. The great thing with God is that He even helps us get back on the road if we've wandered off. His grace and forgiveness is like a tow truck that can pull you out of the ditch and back onto the road. Psalm 25:4-5 says, "Show me your ways, LORD, teach me your paths. Guide me in your truth and teach me, for you are God my Savior, and my hope is in you all day long."

Dear God, thank You for giving me clear guidelines and direction for my life. I'm so grateful that You care enough about me to help me. If I have veered off the road in some area of my life, like with my friends or some of the choices I make, can You show me how to get back on the road? In Jesus's name, amen.

The Trust Game

Have you ever played the trust game? This is when you stand in front of someone with your back to him or her, cross your arms, and fall backward into their arms and hope they catch you! *If you have never done this before, be sure to ask an adult before you try it!* The trust game is a lot of fun—well, as long as you trust or believe that the person standing behind you will catch you! It is not so fun if you cannot trust them because you may actually hurt yourself when you fall.

What if God was the person standing behind you? Would you trust that He would catch you or would you be too afraid to fall?

Let me give you some good news. You can always trust God. Sometimes it may feel like you are falling backward and are headed for the ground, but do not be afraid. God will not let you fall.

Trusting God is hard because you do not always know or understand what He is doing or what He has planned for you. It may seem like He is not standing there, but trust Him anyway! God always takes care of you.

Proverbs 3:5 says, "Trust in the LORD with all your heart and lean not on your own understanding." It is impossible for you and me to understand or think like God. He always has a plan better than anything you can even imagine! Trust Him with your entire heart and with every part of your life. You can trust that God will help you to choose good friends. You can trust that He will help you pass or do well on a test or in a job. You can also even trust that when things look or feel bad, God is waiting, ready to catch you! Fall into His arms and trust that He will be with you and help you no matter what!

Dear God, I am so glad that You are always ready to catch me. Help me to feel safe and know You are there for me, even when I don't see You. In Jesus's name, amen.

Follow the Leader

When you are with your friends, do you enjoy being in charge and making up the rules to a new game? Do you like giving everyone their instructions on how to play? Or would you rather see what others are doing and help them with what they need?

I bet you enjoy a little bit of both—leading others in some ways and helping out in others! Whichever you enjoy the most, do not feel bad about it! Leading and following are very important and both are needed.

Every team needs a coach and every coach needs a team, right? Could there even be a soccer team without a coach? Or what good is a coach without the team? It just could not work! They both need each other in order to play.

Being able to lead others is a gift, and being able to work well with other people is a gift too. In Matthew 20:26 Jesus says, "Whoever wants to become great among you must be your servant." Think about Jesus, the Son of God. Jesus is always our example and the Bible says that He is both a leader and a servant. As God's Son, He is in charge but He leads by helping others.

The next time you are trying to get your friends or little brothers or sisters to do something, do not just boss them around! Be patient.

Show them how to do it and think of how you can help them.

How can you lead by serving today?

Dear God, help me to lead. Help me to follow. Thank You for teaching me that serving others is how I start being a leader. In Jesus's name, amen.

Money

When I was a little girl, I remember being very upset because my mom told me she could not buy me what I asked for. She told me that she did not have the money to pay for it and that "money does not grow on trees!"

Well, of course I knew that money did not grow on trees. How weird would that be? But I did not understand why she could not get me what I wanted. Now I know that my mom only had a certain amount of money and that she could not spend it all on me. She had to be careful about how she spent her money.

Do you have a bank—a bottle, a pig, or some other fun shape that you keep full of coins? A bank is a safe place to keep your money and helps you to save it. You may not have a job yet, and you may not have a lot of money right now, but starting to think about how you spend your money is still a good idea.

In Matthew 6:21 Jesus says, "For where your treasure is, there your heart will be also." This means that you will spend your money on the things that mean the most to you—the things you value. What means the most to you? When you earn money for doing a special job or even as a gift, do you spend it all right away? What do you buy?

There is nothing wrong with buying fun

things, but be sure that that is not all you use your money for. Think about others, your future, and God when you have to decide how to spend your money. The money you have is not yours; it belongs to God. He gave it to you and He wants you to be smart in how you use it.

Dear God, when I earn money or receive it as a gift, help me to remember that You gave it to me for a reason. Help me to practice being wise in how I spend. In Jesus's name, amen.

Here is a good way to be sure that you are on the right track when spending your money!

1. Give to God first through your church or by asking God to show you who you might help with the money He has given you.

2. Save some for later. You never know when you might need something.

3. Spend a little on yourself! But not until after you have made sure to put God first and your future second. It is always more fun to get a treat when you know you were wise with the money God gave you.

Who Is Responsible?

Are you a responsible person? Do you do what you say you are going to do when you say you are going to do it? Do you take care of your things and help your family around the house? I hope so, because being responsible is very important. One day you are going to be responsible for a lot more than just your toys!

Think about it. When you are a teenager, will you want to have a phone or drive a car? How about when you get even older? Will you want to live in your own apartment? These things may seem too far away to think about, but the way you practice taking care of your things now will shape how responsible you will be later. When you get older, you are going to want people to trust you to make good decisions. Do you think your mom will let you drive her car if you can't even take care of your socks? Probably not!

In Luke 16:10 Jesus says, "Whoever can be trusted with very little can also be trusted with much, and whoever is dishonest with very little will also be dishonest with much." Being responsible means that people can trust you to do what you say you are going to do and to take care of what you have. It is also a great way to show that you are grateful for the things you have been given.

You may forget to pick up your shoes or put away your books every once in a while, but if you are responsible you will do it as soon as you notice that you forgot! That means that you don't cry or stomp when you are reminded to do what you need to do but instead you quickly take care of it.

How can you be responsible today?

Dear God, thank You for everything You've given me. Help me take care of it all. I want people to trust that I will do what I say I am going to do. Will You help me be a responsible person? In Jesus's name, amen.

Obedience

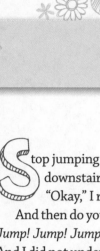

"Stop jumping on the bed!" my mother yelled to me from downstairs.

"Okay," I replied.

And then do you know what I did next? I finished jumping. *Jump! Jump! Jump!* I was having way too much fun to stop! And I did not understand why she wanted me to stop jumping anyway. I did not think it really mattered! Now, do you know what happened next?

You got it. My mother stormed upstairs! She was very disappointed with my behavior. She explained to me that jumping on the bed can be dangerous because I could fall off and hurt myself. The fun was over.

Have you ever had something like this happen to you? Maybe you have done something you knew was against the rules, but you really did not think it mattered. Maybe you took an extra cookie after your mom told you not to. Or instead of cleaning your room when you were told, you decided to stuff all of the mess into your closet. You may think that these things are not a big deal. Who cares about one cookie or a messy closet?

Well, God does. God cares about your obedience. Even if you do not understand how your disobedience can affect other people, you should always do your best to always obey. God wants you to obey Him, your parents, your teachers, and other people that He has put in charge over you. You may not understand the results of your choices, but God does. Just like my mother was trying to protect me from the pain of falling off the bed, God wants to protect you from future trouble.

Being obedient is not always easy, but God wants to help you. Just ask Him! Pray this verse from the Psalms: "Teach me to do your will, for you are my God; may your good Spirit lead me on level ground" (Psalm 143:10).

Dear God, thank You for dying for my disobedience so I wouldn't have to. Please help me know You more. Teach me to obey You and my parents. In Jesus's name, amen.

Change

Change is inevitable. Can you say that? *Inevitable* is a fancy word that means something cannot be stopped. Change cannot be stopped. At some point, something around you will change. The weather changes, your shoe size changes, and even your favorite color will probably change. (Okay, maybe not that!)

Some changes are fun and exciting, like your birthday! Each year your age changes and that even starts off with fun, yummy cake! Other changes may make you sad, like having to move to a new school or a new house. Saying goodbye to old friends is never easy.

Can you think of a time when something changed in your life? How did you feel about the change you had to make? Were you afraid or excited?

Well, I have some good news for you. When everything else is changing around you, there is one thing that will not. God. When everything around you is changing, He stays just as good and just as awesome! He tells us in Malachi 3:6, "I the LORD do not change."

I bet you have already seen a lot of change in your life. Some good and some not so good. There are two things that I can promise you. The first is that change will keep coming. The second is good news: God stays the same as things change.

When you are going through change, always remember to look to God's Word. In the good and the bad He will be with you and His Word will guide you. Trust that He is doing what is best for you. Every change is a new opportunity to see what else God has planned for your life!

Dear God, thank You for letting me know that You do not change and I can depend on You when things are changing in my life. Help me to look to You and the Bible as my guide. When things around me change, help me believe that You are still the same. In Jesus's name, amen.

Don't Be Afraid

Is there anything you're afraid of? Maybe you are afraid of being in a dark room alone or of flying on an airplane. Maybe you are afraid of meeting new people or speaking in front of a big group of strangers.

Whatever it is that you are afraid of, remember that it is nothing to be embarrassed about, but there is something you can do to help! You can pray and ask God to help you.

God does not want you to be afraid of anything! He does not give you fear—and He's given you a few other things instead. Second Timothy 1:7 says, "the Spirit God gave us does not make us timid, but gives us power, love and self-discipline."

So let's talk about your fear. Have you noticed that fear does not always make sense? For example, you may be afraid of bugs. So am I! But why? They are smaller than us, they do not have the same brains as we do, and most of all they can only do what God makes them do. The truth is that God will take care of us—even if we get stung or bitten by a bug!

Fear can keep you from trying new things and it can stop you from doing everything God has planned for you to do. That is not what God wants, and I am pretty sure that is not what you want either! Your feelings may say that you should be afraid, but God says different! If you fill your mind with God's truth, it becomes easier to trust Him even when you feel afraid.

Whatever it is you are afraid of, decide right now to give it to God and ask Him to replace your fear with His power and His love!

Dear God, sometimes I feel afraid. I know that You do not want me to feel fear, so will You help me? Help me think of Your love for me whenever I feel scared. In Jesus's name, amen.

Cleaning Up

If you took a bath with muddy water, do you think you would you get very clean?

I don't want you to do this, but I am pretty sure that no matter how hard you tried, you could not clean yourself with a bathtub full of dirty water. You would actually be doing the opposite. The more you wiped with it, the dirtier you would make yourself!

Now, do you think anyone would want to do that?

Well, bathing with muddy water is something people do all the time. You must think I am crazy but let me ask you a question. When you make mistakes or bad choices, do you try to fix them by working more and trying harder to be better? Have you ever noticed that no matter how hard you try, you just keep making more and more mistakes?

Trying to make yourself do and be better is like bathing with muddy water. God does want you to always try your best and do your best, but He knows that without Him your best is like taking a muddy bath. You will never get clean on your own. You just don't have what you need, and the harder you try without God, well, the dirtier you will get.

The Bible says Jesus is the only one who can make you clean! I am not talking about having a clean body anymore, but Jesus wants to give you a clean heart. When King David was feeling really dirty from some things he had done wrong, he wrote this prayer to God: "Create in me a pure heart, O God, and renew a steadfast spirit within me" (Psalm 51:10).

There are times when your heart becomes dirty with things like anger, jealousy, negativity, or dishonesty. These things are sinful and the only person that can clean you up from them is God! God wants to bathe you in His love and His grace. His love is like the cleanest water you'll ever bathe in!

Dear God, I can't take away all my sins on my own. Please wash me clean—as white as snow! Make my heart clean today. In Jesus's name, amen.

What's So Funny?

Do you ever feel like God is only interested in the really serious things in your life? Maybe you don't think that God likes to have fun and laugh, or maybe you have never even thought about it. Well, the Bible says that God is the reason for all joy and fun. He loves it when you have good times and experience His joy and happiness.

Seriously! Who do you think created smiles, giggles, and laughter anyway? God did! And it is something He talks about in His Word. The Bible says that when you think about how good God is, He will fill you with more joy and gladness than you can imagine! Psalm 32:11 says, "Rejoice in the LORD and be glad, you righteous; sing, all you who are upright in heart!"

Real joy will make you laugh. Laughter makes you feel better and it makes the people around you feel better, on the outside and on the inside. Sometimes it can even be contagious! That means that if you start laughing at something, someone else around you will probably start to do the same thing.

Do what God says often—be glad and laugh! Even when everything is not going the way you want it to, think about how much God loves you and how good He is. Let His love fill your heart with joy...and of course fill your mouth with laughter!

Loud and crazy or soft and cute, only God could make something as cool as laughter!

Dear God, thank You for laughter! I love that You want me to have joy. Help me remember how good You are to me and help me share my joy and laughter with other people! In Jesus's name, amen.

Brush Daily

How often do you brush your teeth? Hopefully you said at least twice a day, every day! Some people brush their teeth after every meal. They even bring their toothbrush to school! They know that the more they brush, the healthier their teeth will be.

Why do you brush your teeth? What do you think would happen if you only brushed them once a week or once a month? If you let food and germs stay on your teeth, they would be ruined and could not be used to help you chew, talk, or smile. Being able to do these things is pretty important! So in the morning and in the evening you head to the bathroom, stand over the sink, and put a little toothpaste on your brush. You work hard to take care of your teeth and to protect them.

Now let me ask you a question. How important is your relationship with God? How often do you talk to Him? Do you talk to Him at least twice a day? Hopefully you talk to Him even more than that!

Prayer is like brushing your teeth. The more you do it, the better the results. If you only pray once a week, like at church on Sundays, your relationship with God may not be so fresh! Talking to God often is a way for you to protect yourself and brush away the lies and hurtful things that are all around you every day. These things destroy your relationship with God and stop you from doing the important things He wants you to do.

Unlike brushing your teeth, you don't have to pray in a certain place or a certain way. You can talk to God anywhere at any time that you need to! First Thessalonians 5:17 says it best: "Pray continually."

Dear God, I'm so glad I can talk to You as often as I want! Help me to remember how important it is to pray so that I can stay fresh and shiny and have a better friendship with You for my whole life! In Jesus's name, amen.

Serving Makes Bad Days Better

I am going to tell you something that you may have never even thought about. When you are having a bad day, you should find a way to help brighten someone else's day! Serving other people will make you feel better.

It is true! One of the reasons bad days feel so bad is because you probably spend all day thinking and talking about just how bad your day is and all the things that are wrong with your life. If this is all you think about then it is all you will talk about and, well, nothing will make your day better.

But if you stop thinking about yourself and think of ways to make someone else smile, your bad day can change! Helping someone else will quickly get your focus off yourself and your problems.

Jesus's life is a shining example of this very thing. We can all agree that Jesus had a few things happen to Him that could have led to bad days. From the time Jesus was born, He knew that He would have to die and be punished for the mistakes and sins of others, including you and me. Jesus could have cried and complained about this every day! But He did not. Instead, He served others. He healed people, looked for ways to change lives, and kept doing what God told Him to do.

Matthew 20:28 tells us that "the Son of Man did not come to be served, but to serve, and to give his life as a ransom for many."

You will not always have great days. But you will always have a chance to make someone else's day better. No matter what you feel like or what may be happening, look for ways to serve. It can be helping a little brother tie his shoe, smiling at someone who looks sad, or even telling a teacher, "Thank you." These are all great ways to serve! Ask God to help you see all the opportunities to serve—and to make those bad days better.

Dear God, when I only think about me it is easy to only see things that aren't going my way. Help me to focus on others, and make my day brighter as I do! In Jesus's name, amen.

Sometimes it takes very little to make a huge change! Talk to your family and see who you may be able to help. There are probably people in your church, school, or even in your own home who could use your service in some way!

A few things to consider:

- Help a little brother or sister with homework.
- Bake cookies for a friend.
- Pick up trash in your neighborhood.
- Write a letter to someone in the military.
- Visit people in the hospital.

This list could go on and on. Add a few ideas and choose which ones you want to do!

Love Who He Is

God loves to take care of His children. He enjoys His creation. The Bible describes Him as being kind, giving, and wonderful. He just cannot help but to be these things because He is love!

Because of all the wonderful things that God does, everyone always talks about how good God is and all the great and amazing things that He has given them. God wants you to be grateful for the ways He shows His love for you, but He does not want you to love Him for what He can do for you. He wants you to love Him for who He is!

If you had a friend who only wanted to come over and play when you got a new toy, how would you feel? Suppose you invited them over a lot but they never seemed to come unless you told them there was something new and cool to do. I bet you would probably feel sad and think your friend only liked you for the things that you have.

This is what it's like if you only talk to God or about Him to others when He gives you something new or you need His help with something. God does not want this. God has many blessings He wants to give you and He loves to help you, but He wants you to love Him even if He didn't give you anything new!

Think about it. If God did not give you

anything else for the rest of your life, would you still love Him?

You may be wondering how you know if you love God for who He is. John 14:15 says, "If you love me, keep my commands." This does not mean God wants you to prove your love for Him by doing what He says. It just means that you will know that you love Him for who He is when you think about Him before you do something. He wants you to love Him so much that you are always looking for things to do for Him instead of only looking for what He is going to do for you!

Dear God, I love You so much. Help me to love You more today than I did yesterday and more tomorrow than I do today. Help me to obey You because I love You, and show me how to love You more. In Jesus's name, amen.

Don't Pop!

What happens when you blow air into a balloon? It gets bigger and bigger, right? Some balloons can get bigger than others because they can stretch more and hold more air. The air in the balloon pushes and pushes against the inside of the balloon until it just has nowhere else to go. That's when you hear that loud sound that surprises and scares everyone and then you see pieces of the balloon flying across the room.

Pop!

Have you ever felt like a balloon? Have you ever felt like you had too much inside your head and you had to let it out? You probably do not get full of air, but there are many things that your brain and your heart can get full of. Things like sadness, anger, fear, or even just a lot of questions. Do you keep these things inside or do you have a way to let some of them out?

God wants you to have room in your heart for Him to keep putting more and more of His goodness inside. That means that you have to let some of the other things out in order to make sure you don't "pop!"

If you ever feel that you are getting too full of bad emotions or feelings, always take time to talk to God about it—as well as a good friend, a parent, a pastor, or someone you can trust. You may not want to talk about how you feel or what you are holding inside, but the Bible says that it is wise to listen to advice. God can use other people around you to help you. "Listen to advice and accept discipline, and at the end you will be counted among the wise" (Proverbs 19:20).

Is your heart full of bad thoughts or emotions today? Ask God to help you let some things out.

Dear God, sometimes my heart and brain can get so full of things that do not feel good. I know that I can always talk to You, but I know that sometimes I need to talk to someone else. Will You help me talk to someone about how I am feeling? Will You help me know who I can trust to share my feelings with? In Jesus's name, amen.

The "G" Word

One of the best things about having friends is that you have other people to talk to. A good conversation with friends is sometimes the one thing you need to make you smile, right?

There are so many fun and wonderful things you can talk to your friends about. You can talk about what movies you like, your favorite outfits, and the most recent books you have read. You can talk about homework, your teachers, and your classmates. When friends get together there are hours of conversations and giggles waiting to happen!

But when you talk to your friends, there is something you have to be careful not to do. Let's call it the "G" word. You might know it. *Gossip*.

Gossip is when someone talks about another person in a way that is untrue or hurtful. Gossip can get a little tricky, and here is why: Gossip is not just about what you say. It is also about what you hear. What you listen to and let other people say about others is just as important as what you say.

Leviticus 19:16 says, "Do not go about spreading slander among your people." God does not want His children to gossip. Nope. So be careful not to let unpleasant or untrue words about other people come out of your mouth, or go into your ears! He even wants you to help stop gossip if you are able to.

As God's girl, you have to protect yourself and the people around you—and gossip is hurtful to everyone.

Here are a few things to think about when you and your friends start to talk: Are the things you are saying about other people true? Are you saying things that are helpful and kind? Are you speaking in love? If someone heard what you were saying, would they know that you loved them?

If you can answer "no" to any of these questions, then it's time to change the conversation! With so many fun things to talk about, be sure to say things that would bring a smile to God!

Dear God, thank You for my friends and the people I get to talk to every day. Help me not to gossip and give me the courage I need to stop others from gossiping when I hear them. Help me to look like You, even when I am having fun talking to my friends. In Jesus's name, amen.

I Am a Temple

There are probably many things happening to your body right now. Your feet are growing. Your legs are getting stronger. Your arms are getting longer. Your teeth are falling out and coming back, and they are even bigger than before!

The list could go on and on, because I am sure that there are many things growing and changing on your body. As you get older your body will continue to change. One day your hair may turn white and your face will get wrinkles!

It can be a little strange and scary when it starts to happen. But you do not have to be afraid or embarrassed because God knows what He is doing. Psalm 139:14 says, "I praise you because I am fearfully and wonderfully made." No matter what is happening on the outside of your body, you can remember that God lives on the inside. The Bible says your body is God's temple.

When you think of the word *temple*, you may only think of churches and buildings where people go to praise God. You are definitely not a big building, but God says your body is a place where He lives and is worshipped. Think about the building where you go to church. Do you throw trash around on the inside of it or do you do your best to take care of it?

That is exactly how God always wants you to

treat your body. Do you treat your body like a
temple? If not, then start today! Thank God
for making you His temple.

Dear God, thank You for the way You made my
body. As I continue to grow and change, help me
remember that my body is Yours. I want to think
of myself as a temple, a special place where You
live. I'm so glad You live inside me. In Jesus's name,
amen.

Rules Are Good

When I was a little girl, I always wanted to be like my older cousins. They got to stay up later than me, wear makeup, see movies I couldn't see, choose what they wanted to wear, and even drive! It just wasn't fair that they did not have the same rules as I did and that they did not have so many people telling them what to do all the time.

I just could not wait to be older!

There is something about being a teenager or an adult that looks really cool. On television shows, walking around the mall, and at school, they are always having so much fun hanging out with their friends. Maybe it's the clothes they wear, their attitude, or their makeup that makes them look so awesome.

Do you ever feel like this? Do you ever want to be older? Maybe you think that the older you get, the more fun you will be able to have because you will get to be your own boss! That's what I thought too. And then I learned the truth. Want to know it? Although it looks like teenagers and adults don't have many rules to follow, no matter how old you get, there is always someone else in charge and rules to follow. There will be laws in the cities where you live, a boss on your job where you work, and (most important) God's rules.

Even if you do not like what they say, God wants you to always obey the people that have authority or power over you. He also wants you to do it with a good attitude! That means you shouldn't pout if you have to go to bed earlier than someone else or throw a tantrum when you can't go somewhere or do something. Hebrews 13:17 says, "Have confidence in your leaders and submit to their authority, because they keep watch over you."

What is one rule that you wish you did not have to follow? Thank God for it anyway and pray that He helps you understand and obey it!

Dear God, thank You for loving me enough to give me rules. Sometimes it does not feel good to be told what to do or what not to do, but help me remember that rules are there to protect me, not hurt me. In Jesus's name, amen.

Gravity

Life would be different if you lived in outer space. I am sure of it! When astronauts go into space, they have to get used to a few things—like riding in a spaceship and wearing a spacesuit! Can you imagine having to wearing a suit like that all day and all night? They also have to get used to floating around in the air. Think about it. If you were to live in space, it would be really hard for you to sit down for dinner, play a game of soccer, or lie down for a nap because there is no gravity. Gravity is the force that keeps you on the ground. Without it you do not have much control of your body.

Floating around may look like fun, but can you imagine what it would feel like not to be able to keep yourself or the things around you down on the ground? Not being able to make your body stay still or sit would be a little weird, wouldn't it?

The Bible says being grounded is a good thing! Not just for your body, but for your heart and your mind. Ephesians 3:17 says that when Christ dwells in our hearts, we are "rooted and established in love." This means that God's love in your heart is like the gravity in your life. No matter what may be going on around you, having God's love in your heart will hold you in place. His love is stronger than anything!

Do you ever feel like you may "float" away because of something happening around you? Maybe you keep arguing with your mom or there is chaos at school. These things can be hard to handle, but remember that God's love is stronger. Pray and ask Him to keep you standing on the ground!

Dear God, thank You for Your love in my heart! Help me remember that I do not have to be overwhelmed by what is happening around me because Your love is strong and it is in me! In Jesus's name, amen.

Watch It Grow

Can you tell me the one thing that your fingernails do? Fingernails grow! No matter how short yours may be, give them some time and they will grow. Even if you keep biting them off they will just keep coming back!

But have you actually seen a fingernail grow? Think about it, when is the last time you sat down, laid your hand on the table and tried to watch your fingernails grow, even a centimeter?

I am thinking you said, "Never!" That is because it is pretty impossible. Staring at your fingernails and waiting to see them grow would probably drive you bananas! You may be sitting there for a very, very, very long time.

But do you have faith that they will grow? I bet you do. That is why you just keep wanting new, fun, and colorful fingernail polish to paint them with! To have faith means that you believe something is true or that something will happen, even if you do not see it. In Hebrews 11:1, God explains faith like this: "Now faith is confidence in what we hope for and assurance about what we do not see."

Did you know that having a relationship with God means you have faith in Him? Even though you have never seen God, you have to believe that He is real and He is working in your life! Just like you want to keep buying more and more fingernail polish, keep loving God and wanting more of Him in your life!

Are you waiting for something to happen? What are things you cannot see but you need to believe God for? God wants you to have faith in Him. He promises to take care of you!

Dear God, thank You for wanting to take care of me. As I keep getting to know You, help me to believe that You are real and to have faith in You! In Jesus's name, amen.

Pray for Others

If you could guess how many people you see in a day, what would you say? You can start with your best girlfriends, add your classmates, and keep on going from there! You really can count if you want to, but I think the answer to the question is…a lot!

If you talk to your friends every day, you probably know a lot about their lives. You know when they are sad and when they are really happy about something. You also know if they need help or advice.

What do you do when your friends decide to tell you about their problems? Hopefully you listen to them and try to help them feel better, but God wants you to do even more than that. God wants you to do something really big for the people you get to talk to. Do you know what that is? God wants all people to know Him, and He wants to use you to help make sure that happens!

One of the most important things you can do for your friends is to pray for their relationship with God. It is also the most important thing you can do for people you don't even know! If you're not sure what to say, try repeating the words of Paul when he prayed for people in a place called Ephesus:

"I keep asking that the God of our Lord Jesus Christ, the glorious Father, may give you the

Spirit of wisdom and revelation, so that you may know him better. I pray that the eyes of your heart may be enlightened in order that you may know the hope to which he has called you, the riches of his glorious inheritance in his holy people" (Ephesians 1:17-18).

Isn't that the best prayer to pray for someone else? What a good prayer to pray for your best friends and for everyone else! Today, pray that your friends and all people would get to know God better!

Dear God, thank You that I can talk to You about anything and everything. Remind me to pray for my friends and others who need to know You better. In Jesus's name, amen.

Choose a friend or two to pray this prayer for.

Dear God, may You give _____ the Spirit of wisdom and revelation, so that she may know You better. I pray that the eyes of _____'s heart may be enlightened in order that she may know the hope to which You have called her, the riches of Your glorious inheritance in Your holy people.

How Do You Feel?

How do you feel? Believe it or not, that can be a really tricky question! So before you answer, I want you to think about it carefully. Right now, how do you feel in your heart and in your mind, not in your body? Has something happened today to make you feel the way you do right now? Maybe you are happy, excited, sad, confused, nervous, or even a mix of these things.

These feelings are called emotions, and guess what? We all have them! Your emotions are the way you feel and they change depending on what is happening around you. Emotions can make you want to act a certain way. For example, crying is one of the ways you can show your emotions. If you are feeling excited, you may want to smile and jump! But if you are feeling angry you may want to yell and scream.

You do not have to be embarrassed by your emotions, but you do have to be careful with them. The way that you feel is important, but you cannot let emotions or your feelings control your behavior or how you act. You can really be sad because you failed a test or because someone said something mean to you. But you cannot let your sad feelings make you do something that God would not want you to do!

Feelings do not always lead you where God wants you. They aren't always true. Yep, they can lie to you! They can also change from situation to situation and are unpredictable.

Proverbs 3:5-6 says, "Trust in the LORD with all your heart and lean not on your own understanding; in all your ways submit to him, and he will make your paths straight." No matter what you may be feeling, trust God! Being sad, mad, or glad are real feelings. You will have bad ones. You will have happy ones. But no matter what your emotions and feelings are today, ask God to help you make good decisions and have good thoughts.

Dear God, thank You for my emotions and my feelings. Thank You that I can feel happy, glad, and even silly. When I'm sad or mad or have feelings that could be hurtful, help me think about You. In Jesus's name, amen.

Keep Doing It

I love to dance! Dancing is one of my favorite things to do. But there's just one problem…I'm not very good at it. I think I hear different music in my head from what is actually being played. When everyone is going in a certain direction, I am the one going the opposite way. Arms flying, legs wiggling, and not really dancing at all! I look much more like an excited puppy than an elegant ballerina.

When I was a little girl, I used to wish I could dance like some of my friends. They were really good at it and, well, I was not. I always wanted to be on the dance team at school, but I never even tried out. I never took dance classes because I just knew there was no way anyone could help me learn to dance better.

I was so embarrassed by my dance moves that eventually I just stopped dancing. Well, I stopped dancing in front of other people. When music would come on, I would just stand still and try really hard to hold in my fancy moves! But it was hard to not dance because dancing brings me joy. One day, I just could not hold it in anymore! I started dancing and I did not even care how silly I looked. I started dancing all over the place! And do you know what? My friends didn't care either. No one laughed at me or even asked me to stop! They were just happy that I was having fun with them.

Now I wonder what would have happened if I had tried out for the team or taken a class. I know I would have had a lot of fun, even if I did not learn to dance perfectly.

Is there something that you love doing but think you are not that good at? Well, don't stop doing it! Never let what others think, or even what you *think* they will think, stop you from trying and doing things you love. You may not look or sound like the people around you, but remember, that is just because God made you unique. Have fun, try new things, and do what makes your heart happy!

First Corinthians 10:31 reminds us, "Whether you eat or drink or whatever you do, do it all for the glory of God." As long as you can say you were doing it for God's glory, you can do it with joy and a smile! When you dance or sing or paint or whatever, ask yourself, *Would God smile if He saw me?* If you can answer *yes*, keep on doing it!

Dear God, I know there are people who are better than me at _____, but I love doing it. Help me to keep on doing it! Help me to make You look awesome and give You glory as I try. In Jesus's name, amen.

Have you ever felt like God had something special He wanted you to do? Maybe you were sitting next to a classmate who was having a hard time understanding a math problem. Or you walked by when a friend was alone crying in the hallway. Do you think that just happened by accident? Or do you think that maybe God chose you to be the person there at that time?

God does everything on purpose! If you are the one who walks in when someone needs help, you should be sure to ask God how you can help him or her. He chose you to be there! God wants to use you to help others. It is true! God loves using His children. You are never too old or too young for God to use you. He always has a plan.

And do you know what else? The Bible is full of stories of God using girls just like you to do something special for other people.

One of the most popular stories in the Bible is the story of Queen Esther. Esther was not born a queen. She was born a regular girl like you and me. But God chose her to marry a king! She became the queen and God used her to save a lot of lives. This was God's plan all along. God chose Esther to be where she was when He needed her to help save others. You can read the whole story in the book of Esther if you'd like.

There are many other stories just like Esther's. You may not become a queen, but every day God puts you in a place where He can use you in some way. He wants you to be ready and willing to let Him.

Today, remember to keep your eyes open for how God will use you. Do not miss your chance today!

Dear God, thank You for choosing me to be the one You want to use. Help me be ready for everything that You have for me today! I want You to use me. In Jesus's name, amen.

The Bible is full of many wonderful girls and women, and some of them were not much older than you! There are even books of the Bible named after girls God used to do something special.

Take time to read their stories and journal about what you learn. Always remember that God wants to use your life too! Read the books of Ruth and Esther. You may want to use a study Bible to find out even more about these incredible young women. A study Bible has special notes and information that help you understand more about the stories you are reading.

Find Him

Have you ever been lost? Maybe you were driving with your mom and trying to find your friend's birthday party. Or maybe it was your first day at a new school and you were walking around looking for the right classroom but you just couldn't find it.

Maybe this has never happened to you, but it happens to me all of the time! Can you believe I even get lost when I have directions? I always try to leave early when I am going somewhere new because I know I will probably spend a lot of time driving in circles looking for the right place. I have to remind myself to be very patient.

Being lost can be very frustrating—especially if you really have to be somewhere or people are waiting for you. No matter how lost you are, remember that it does not mean that you have to turn around and go home. The place you are looking for is still there, so you just have to keep trying to find it! Sometimes you may just need to ask someone else to help you get there.

Do you know that sometimes you can even feel lost in your relationship with God? You may be trying really hard to get closer to Him, but it just doesn't seem to work. Maybe you are doing your best to do the right things—like reading your Bible and praying—but you still feel like you can't find Him.

Don't turn around and don't give up! Pray and ask God to help you get closer to Him. Deuteronomy 4:29 says, "If...you seek the LORD your God, you will find him if you seek him with all your heart and with all your soul." God wants you to remember that He is always there! He wants you to look for Him. Be patient. He does not mind waiting for you and promises to help you find Him when you look for Him with all of your heart!

Dear God, I love You and want to know You more. I commit to looking for You with all my heart, because I know You are reaching out to me. In Jesus's name, amen.

Identity

Do you know who you are?

Well, of course. You know your name, where you live, and who your parents are. You know what you like to do, and you definitely know what you don't like doing! These things are all very important and they definitely help you to be fabulous and awesome...but I want to know about your true identity.

Know what makes you special? You are God's daughter!

You are valuable.

You are loved.

You are God's special creation!

Remembering these things is a big deal because knowing your identity helps you out when you are making decisions. This is why God wants you to know that your identity is in Him! You are who He says you are...even if your friends or family say something different. When you know that you are God's daughter, you care about what He thinks and you want to please Him!

Galatians 2:20 says, "I have been crucified with Christ and I no longer live, but Christ lives in me. The life I now live in the body, I live by faith in the Son of God, who loved me and gave himself for me."

If you are God's girl, then this verse is true for

you! If you have put your trust in Jesus then He lives in you and He is your identity!

Dear God, help me remember that I am Your child. You are my identity and I am only who You say I am! I am Yours. In Jesus's name, amen.